Published in 2017 by
Moira Brown
Broughty Ferry
Dundee. DD5 2HZ
www.publishkindlebooks4u.co.uk

Via Suez was first published
as a kindle book in 2013.

Copyright © Ian M. Malcolm

The right of Ian M. Malcolm to be identified as the Author
of this work has been asserted in accordance with the
Copyrights, Designs and Patents Act 1988.

All rights reserved. No part of this book may be reprinted or reproduced or utilised in any form or by any electronic, mechanical or other means, now known or hereafter invented, including photocopying or recording, or any information storage or retrieval system, without the permission in writing from the Publisher.

ISBN 978-1-5215-0267-9

VIA SUEZ

Ian M. Malcolm

1	FORCIBLY (RE)PROMOTED AND SHIPMATES	1
2	SHIPMATES	3
3	VOYAGE 7 OF THE GLENGARRY BEGINS	6
4	TYPHOON	9
5	JAPAN	12
6	THE HOMEWARD RUN BEGINS	15
7	CHRISTMAS 1949	17
8	COLOMBO TO ADEN	21
9	ADEN TO ALEXANDRIA	24
10	GENOA AND HOME	27
11	REJOINING AGAIN	33
12	SHIPMATES	37
13	VOYAGE 8 OF THE GLENGARRY BEGINS	40
14	PORT SAID TO MALAYA	43
15	HONG KONG	49
16	TAKU BAR	51
17	JAPAN	54
18	HONG KONG HOMEWARD	56
19	MALAYA	77
20	THE LAST LEG	83
21	LONDON INTERLUDE	87
22	SHIPMATES	89
23	CONTINENTAL PORTS AND HOME	91
24	COASTING THE ELPENOR /GLENFINLAS	95
25	COASTING THE HELENUS	103

26	**COASTING THE PATROCLUS**	106
27	**COASTING THE MEDON**	109
28	**LOOKING FOR A SHIP**	116
29	**COASTING THE CLYTONEUS**	121

1   FORCIBLY (RE)PROMOTED AND SHIPMATES

I was employed by Alfred Holt & Co., owners of the Blue Funnel Line and the Glen Line and had made two voyages on the *Glengarry* as 2nd Radio Officer. Previous to that, I had sailed as 1st R/O, but had reverted to 2nd on request. This was because the No.1's job was much more onerous and time-consuming than that of the 2nd R/O as, in addition to being responsible for the wireless room, he was the ship's purser, and I wanted time to study for City and Guilds certificates.

After over three weeks' leave, I was expecting a telegram from Holts recalling me to the *Glengarry* in London, as had been done on the previous occasion. But, when the telegram arrived, it instructed me to report to the Liverpool Office and I could not understand this.

When I presented myself before Calverley, at the long desk in the Steamship Department, he went straight into the attack. "I know", he said " that you don't like the purser's work, but Mr White (the No.1 on the previous voyage) has requested leave in order to be married and he can get this only if you are prepared to sail as No.1 again." I was taken aback. "If I do this," I protested, "all the studying I've done will go to waste and I'll have given up the purser's bonus for nothing." "Go and talk it over with Mr. White," said Calverley. In the officers' waiting room, Geoff White, pleaded with me to accept, but I remained adamant. We returned to the desk and Calverley stood looking at me while I made further protestations. But his next words "You're *going* as No.1." put an end to the discussion.

While in the waiting room, I had explained my problem to Joe Florio who was going as Haji Purser on the pilgrim ship *Tyndareus*. He didn't see my point of view and, when he commented that the *Glengarry* was a fine ship, I offered to change places with him. I did this because I thought that, if I had to give up the No.2's job, I might as well enjoy a Haji Purser's higher rate of pay, without the responsibility of the wireless room. But Joe refused the offer.

We were often kept in the waiting room for long periods and would occupy the time by reading through the pile of wartime reports which lay on a small table. These reports, by officers whose ships had been attacked and perhaps sunk, were very interesting and I'm sure that Captain SW Roskill made use of them when writing the Company's Second World War history, "A Merchant Fleet in War". In one of them, a deck officer, while describing the courage of the engineer Victoria Drummond during an action, quite unnecessarily and ungallantly referred to her as having a face like of horse. Victoria Drummond was the first woman to qualify for a (2nd Class) marine engineer's certificate. She never got a British 1st Class certificate, but sailed as Chief Engineer for many years on foreign ships, and died on Christmas Day, 1978 at the age of 84.

During my spell in Liverpool, I lodged at Atlantic House and returned to the Office to receive some instruction in the purser's cargo duties. A clerk asked the name of the ship on which I had previously served as purser and, when I told him it was the *Atreus*, but that he'd find the cargo book useless, he nevertheless located the book before hastily closing it! .

When I rejoined the *Glengarry* in London, it was to find that Gerry Davies, who had been a pal during my first trip on her, was already on board and sailing on her again. Gerry, who was as pleased to see me as I was to see him, said that an uncle of his had a flat in Knightsbridge Mansions and that, as his uncle was not there at the moment, the flat was available for his use. And, when he suggested that we spend the Saturday night there, I readily accepted. Gerry's uncle was the cartoonist Illingsworth of Punch Magazine. The flat was lovely and, to enhance our enjoyment, we had the company of two girls who were trainee nurses at St George's Hospital. One of the girls, whose surname was Prosser, was Gerry's girlfriend from his hometown of Pontypool. And both she and the colleague she brought with her, were extremely well dressed in suits, wore gloves and carried handbags. They made our meal on the Saturday night and certainly surprised me by turning up early on the Sunday morning to make our breakfast. In the afternoon, we had a pleasant walk by the Serpentine in nearby Hyde Park before the girls returned to the hospital and Gerry and I returned to the ship.

2   SHIPMATES

We signed the Articles, opened by Captain Anderson who was not sailing in the ship again, in the saloon on Friday, 30 September, 1949.

54-year-old Captain Duncan MacTavish, a Mull man living in Glasgow, was now Master. He had his Extra Master's Certificate and I had already been with him briefly when coasting the *Machaon* from Glasgow to Birkenhead in April/May, 1948. In spite of his Scottish name, he had a more la-di-dah English accent than any Englishman I ever sailed with, but was a very likeable and considerate man with whom I got on well. His daughter was a doctor and he had her graduation photograph on display in his cabin.

40-year-old Alec Letty, who lived in Largs and had a Master's Certificate, had replaced [1]F.G.C. Jones as 1st Mate. And the first I learned of his drink problem was when he was found to be under the weather as he accompanied the Marine Superintendent's (Captain Baxter Jones') party on their inspection of the ship, the night before we sailed. What a time to choose to display his weakness!

I.R. Atkinson remained as 2nd Mate. A. Rankin, aged 22 and from Glasgow, was 3rd Mate and G.L. Davies, aged 21, returned as Extra 3rd Mate. Both Mr Rankin and Gerry were uncertificated.

Our midshipmen were N.D. Rout, from Liverpool, who was 17 and making his first trip to sea, and R.G. Taylor, aged 19, from Folkestone.

R.E. Molland, the 2nd R/O, lived in Chelsea, and, at 26, was two years older than I was. Dick was born in Peking (Beijing) where his father,

---

[1] On the evening of 15 July, 1950, Mr Jones was on the bridge of the *Glenearn* when she was machine-gunned by Kuomintang 'planes sixty miles north of Keelung. Mr Jones was hit in the chest and thigh and a piece of shrapnel entered his leg. And a Chinese steward received a bullet in the neck. The ship had been bound for Tsingtao, but, due to the seriously injured men, was redirected to Nagasaki from where both were taken by ambulance and then train to a hospital in Kobe. Mr E.T. Briggs, the British Consul at Tamsui on Formosa, received a verbal apology for the attack and the Kuomintang promised compensation to those injured and for damage to the *Glenearn*. The 'planes which attacked the ship were US-built Mustangs and, fortunately, both men recovered from their wounds.

Charles E Molland, was Commissioner of Posts in the Chinese Postal Service. He lived in China - in Shanghai, Chefoo and Wei-hai-wei (the latter two towns on the Shantung Peninsula) - until he was eight when his mother took him and his five-year-old sister to Switzerland because the latter was seriously ill with the whooping cough. Two years later they came to live in Felpham, near Bognor Regis, in Sussex, but were due to reunite with his father in China when the Second World War was declared and their passage on the P & O liner *Canton* (GDDT) was cancelled. The Japanese had invaded China in 1935, but when they entered the war, in December, 1941, Dick's father was placed under house arrest on Shameen Island, near Canton (Kuangchou). And he remained on the island until repatriated to the UK, via Lourenço Marques (Maputo) where the transfer took place, under the Red Cross Civilian Exchange Scheme. Incidentally, Charles Molland served in France as a Captain in the British Army during the First World War when his work was with the Chinese Labour Brigade, a little known civilian unit of manual labourers brought to Europe in Alfred Holt's 'coolie' ships and whose work included the digging of trenches. Dick had served in the RAF during the war, most of the time with the Inter-Services Research Bureau (the Special Operations Executive) and, as a corporal, was eventually placed in charge of their transmitting station at Henley-on-Thames. With the war in Europe over, he was sent to India, in July, 1945, on Shaw Shavill's *Tamaroa* (GFWX), but the Japanese surrendered only days after the ship's arrival in Bombay and he returned home, from Rangoon, on the *Reina del Pacifico* (GMPS). Dick had already made two voyages on the Liberty Ship *Eurymedon* (GBPN), formerly the *Samoa* (BFPF), and although holding only a 2nd Class PMG, possessed a greater knowledge of radio than I did.

W. Topley and W.J. Edwards, again Chief and 2nd Engineers, were the only certificated engineers. 44-year-old I. Jones, a quiet man from Blaenau Festiniog, was Refrigerator Engineer and 26-year-old A.G. Taylor was 3rd. W.K. Ostle, who had been an Assistant on the previous voyage, was now 4th. Of the Assistant Engineers, only R. Boardman remained from the previous voyage and the others were Oldman, Kenworthy, Cole and Moffat; all in their early twenties.

29-year-old V. Lugton, a friendly man from South Shields, was 1st Electrician and 24-year-old C. Green, from Liverpool, was 2nd.

J. Hurst and W.T. Lawless remained as Chief and 2nd Stewards.

Prior to sailing, I was sitting with Mr Hurst in his cabin when a young, first trip, junior engineer came to the door to find out where his cabin was. The lad was dressed in uniform and, after he had gone, Mr Hurst said to me, "Doesn't he have a suit?" Not since the war had Merchant Navy officers worn uniform ashore and, even then, many, and particularly the older ones, had worn 'civvies'. But that young lad could play the piano. I loved to hear him play Beethoven's 'Moonlight Sonata' and he gave me some instruction.

Dr Moloney was again with us, but W.C. Low, aged 35, was now Carpenter.

We carried two Supernumeraries (actually passengers who signed the Articles); E Sayer, who was paid at the nominal rate of 1/- (5p) a month, and was going out to Hong Kong, and 27-year-old J Broomfield, who was to join the *Charon* in Singapore and signed on as Supernumerary 2nd Mate at £45 a month. Now 1st RO/Purser, my basic pay remained at £38, but I had the additional £6 Purser's Bonus as I already had over two years experience in the job. Dick got £28-10/-. The salaries of the Mates were £54, £52, £39 and £37 respectively while those of the engineers were £68, £54, £40, [2]£52 and £33 respectively. Assistant Engineers Oldman and Boardman - £31; the other Assistants - £30. Electricians - £40 and £36. Dr Moloney - £50. Chief and 2nd Stewards - £42-10/- and £32. Carpenter - £39-5/-. Together with our Chinese crew and passengers, we again had in the region of one hundred people on board.

During my spell on the *Glengarry*, the number of passengers carried was reduced from eighteen to twelve. This was because a passenger ship was defined as one which carried more than twelve passengers and required to be surveyed once a year. Holts was first and foremost a cargo company which, before the advent of air travel, provided accommodation primarily for the convenience of those with whom they dealt abroad.

Now that I was No.1 again, I no longer kept a wireless watch.

---

[2] This was the unaccountably high figure shown against Mr Taylor's name on the Articles.

3   VOYAGE 7 OF THE GLENGARRY BEGINS

We sailed from KGV Dock, London at 7.15am on Sunday, 2 October, 1949 and hove to off a town in the English Channel, which may have been Hastings, to calibrate our Lodestone Direction Finder. This was done by Dick and me taking bearings of radio beacons while Mr Letty, the 1st Mate, took visual bearings on a church. To reduce quadrantal error, all domestic aerials were lowered and when we pressed the single stroke gong and noted the radio beacon bearing, Mr Letty, on the monkey island, noted the church bearing on the compass. When the exercise was complete, the mates recorded any difference between D/F and visual bearings which would be taken into consideration in the future. Captain MacTavish was so pleased with our efforts that he came all the way to my cabin to thank me. But, shortly after we were under way again, Mr Letty confessed to me that he had been taking bearings on the wrong church! I respected him for his honesty, but his mistake could be easily rectified.

We anchored in Port Said Harbour at 11.45am on the 10th. We had cargo to discharge and two Arabs, arguing about damaged cargo, came to my cabin to confront me with their problem. "Sir", said one, "he refuses to make the remark," meaning that the other man would not record the damage. I turned to the offender and when I asked if he would just make a small remark, he did and they went away happy. The head stevedore was a heavily built man called Nick and, when damage to light bulbs was reported to me, Dick said that he had seen Nick sitting on them! Two RAF men boarded to ask if we had any cargo for the RAF. I hadn't a clue and it seemed to me that there was so little for them to do that they were given the job of boarding ships from the UK to keep them occupied.

We left Port Said at 11.00am on the 11th and, due to a considerable hold-up of the convoy in the Bitter Lakes, it was 4.18am the next day before we anchored in Suez Bay. We sailed again at 11.18am, anchored off Steamer Point in Aden at 5.18pm on the 15th, and, having bunkered, left at 11.30pm the same day. On 19 October, Dr Moloney inoculated me against cholera.

When I was 1st R/O of the *Atreus*, the cargo manifests had not arrived until Penang, but this time they awaited our arrival at Port Said and Aden, as was the norm, so that, during the crossing of the Indian Ocean, I wrote up the cargo book in readiness for discharging at the outward ports. Due to my stressful experience on the *Atreus*, I was keyed up to make a good job of it although, now on a much faster ship, there was less time to catch up on the work between ports.

We docked at Georgetown, Penang at 6.27am on Monday, 24 October and the discharging, and my hard work, began. Port officials, shore passes and mail had to be dealt and cash paid out to the crew. And, when all this was going on, tally clerks were recording the cargo going over the side and bringing me their tally sheets. We sailed at 4pm the next day. It was only an overnight run to Port Swettenham where it was a repeat performance. We docked there at 7.54am on the 26th and sailed for Singapore at 5.9pm the next day.

France was engaged in its war in Indo-China and when Dick remarked on hearing one of their troopships on the air in the Malacca Strait, I mentioned that I had heard that some of their conscripts were so desperate to escape the conflict that they jumped overboard and tried to swim ashore. Not long afterwards, we heard the ship sending the Urgency Signal XXX followed by 'Man overboard - all ships please keep sharp lookout'.

Similar to Malaya, Indo-China had been occupied by the Japanese and, also similar to Malaya, the Communists led the resistance against the invader. Ho Chi Minh formed the resistance movement, called the Viet Minh, and, when the Japanese were defeated by the Allies in 1945 and the French returned, they began their fight for independence. The People's Republic of China aided them in their struggle while the USA, with its hatred of Communism, gave assistance to the French as they did to the Kuomintang in China. In 1950, China and the USSR recognized the Democratic Republic of Vietnam and, after the defeat of the French at Dien Bien Phu in 1954, the country was divided, at the 17th parallel, into North (Communist) Vietnam and South Vietnam, under French control. The following year, the French withdrew and the independent Republic of (South) Vietnam was established under the Presidency of Ngo Dinh Diem.

Diem's Government, however, was unpopular as it failed to bring about desired reforms and the National Liberation Front, whose aims were to rid the country of foreign troops and the reunification of Vietnam, was formed, in 1960, to oppose the Government. The US became more involved and, after Diem's murder, in 1963, they poured 'advisers' and military equipment into the country and the Vietnam War began. In spite of their military superiority, the bombing of North Vietnam (whose forces supported the Viet Cong, the military wing of the NLF) and the aid of Australian and New Zealand troops, the US lost the war. This was not only because the Viet Cong had the support of the peasants, but because of the antagonism of the American people to such a distant war which claimed the lives of 50000 of their sons. The conflict ended in 1973 and the united country is the Socialist Republic of Vietnam.

We arrived at Pulo Bukum, off Singapore Island, at 6.54am on the 28th and, having bunkered, left at 1.36pm to dock at Main Wharf, in Keppel Harbour, at 2.54pm. Mr Broomfield signed off, to transfer to the *Charon*, the next day. The *Charon* (GZJQ) and her sister ship, the *Gorgon* (MBKC), carried both passengers and livestock on the Singapore/Western Australia run. Both had been built in Dundee, in 1936 and 1933 respectively, and, when I was a boy, I had heard my father speak of them as fine ships when he had worked as an engineering fitter in the Caledon Shipyard. The *Gorgon* was present during the fall of Singapore in February, 1942 and sailed, with 358 refugees on board, three days before the surrender to the Japanese. She was then attacked six times by high-level bombers, but, although she received two direct hits, succeeded in reaching Fremantle.

Being red haired, Dick couldn't stand the hot sun and, when he had a job to do on deck, he stuffed a white handkerchief in the back of his cap to protect his neck. This made him look like a French foreign legionnaire as he surveyed damaged cargo. Our general cargo consisted of everything you could think of from the factories of Britain and, when a case of toys was found to be damaged, a group of us had a fine time making toy frogs jump about in Mr Letty's cabin. Also due to damage, we were able to sample some Dundee cake!

Gerry Davies' girlfriend's brother, doing his National Service in the Army, was stationed in Singapore. He had visited the ship when Gerry and I had made our first voyage together on the *Glengarry* and he visited again. Although the young man was an Oxford graduate, he had been a private on that first occasion, but was now a corporal.

4   TYPHOON

On the afternoon of the day we were due to sail, Dick and I were in the wireless room with the receiver switched on and heard a typhoon warning. The typhoon was heading west across the Philippines and, as it was likely to be in our path, I immediately notified Captain MacTavish. But, although we thought he might postpone our departure, he decided to sail as per schedule and we left the dock at 5.45pm that day, Tuesday, 1 November, 1949.

The weather became increasingly bad as we made our way north through the South China Sea, but, although it appeared obvious that we were heading straight into the typhoon and she was receiving a terrific pounding, the *Glengarry* held her course. Throughout the succeeding days and nights, and irrespective of watch-keeping times, Dick and I copied all the weather reports we could. And I remember copying one from the US Island of Guam. In the shrieking wind and rain, moving about on deck was dangerous. Making his way to the wireless room from his cabin, Dick had to hang on to the handrail along the engine room casing and, when he opened the heavy wooden door of the wireless room, the wind caught it and nearly threw him across the deck. And as he found it impossible to close the door behind him, he hooked it back, closed the inner mesh door and drew the curtain over it to keep out the rain. As I have previously said, the 1st R/O's cabin was adjacent to the wireless room, in an isolated position at the after end of the boat deck. And as my door, like that of the wireless room, led directly onto the deck, I followed Dick's example and left my outer door open on its hook and closed only the inner mesh door. This resulted in my door curtain becoming sodden, but this was preferable to being unable to get out of the room.

The night of 3/4 November was the worst of all. When I entered the wireless during the night, I found a note from Dick saying that our receiving aerial had been carried away and that he had rigged a temporary 'semi-indoor' aerial. Captain MacTavish added to the upheaval by turning the ship round. This manoeuvre put a tremendous strain on the ship; there were crashing noises from all over her and one enormous one from the engine room. But, surprisingly, nobody was hurt. After a few hours steaming south, we turned north again and, throughout our time in the typhoon, we sent weather reports to Hong Kong. It was a frightening time and, although I knew I was on a fine ship, I was very scared indeed. That typhoon wreaked havoc in the Philippines where countless homes were destroyed and hundreds killed. The following morning we put up a new receiving aerial and by Saturday, 5 November, we were through the worst. But it was a relief to dock in Kowloon at 4.18pm that day. When I had occasion to go to Captain MacTavish's quarters during that passage, I found a young woman sitting there while her child, of about two, played on his floor.

Postscript: Although all weather reports sent by shore wireless stations were prefixed 'Typhoon Warning', information provided by the National Meteorological Library and Archive at Bracknell in Berkshire and the Hong Kong Observatory shows that we were in a Tropical Storm and not a typhoon. At noon on 3rd November, the *Glengarry* reported to Hong Kong that the wind speed was about 35 knots, a Force 8 gale on the Beaufort Scale, but, considering the violence of that night, it must have risen to over 55 knots to become Force 11 and a Violent Storm. In the letter I received from Mr KP Wong of the Hong Kong Observatory, he states "The tropical cyclone you came across on 3 November, 1949 did not have a name.....Tropical cyclones were named by the Joint Typhoon Warning Center in Guam, they missed this one." Tropical storms rapidly die out when they reach the mainland and ours hit the coast of Vietnam. Incidentally, on one of my visits to Hong Kong, I went out on deck in the evening to find the harbour absolutely teeming with junks. It was overcast and calm, but, with a storm in the vicinity, they were taking shelter.

When there had been draws at Penang and Singapore, the Agent had brought the cash on board, but, in Hong Kong on this occasion, I had to collect it from Jardine's office in Pedder Street. I was given the money in a brief case and, as it amounted to something equivalent to about £1100 sterling, I held on to that brief case like grim death. Before returning to the ship, however, I bought a postcard to send home, but, when I went into the Post Office to write it and found that I had nothing to write with, I asked a young Chinese lady, by sign language, if I might borrow her pen. She obligingly lent it to me and stood patiently by as I wrote the card while holding the brief case tightly in the other hand. When I thanked the lady, she smiled and said what I took to be "Not at all" in Cantonese.

Most of our cargo was for Hong Kong so that we were there for almost a week and, during our stay, an incident with a Chinese clerk amused me. When I asked when I would receive something or other, he studied his watch and I couldn't understand how looking at a watch would help with the date. But his technology was ahead of mine and this was the first time I came across a watch which showed the date. This man, incidentally, offered me a packet of ginger which I refused on two counts: firstly because Holt's officers were forbidden to accept cumshaw (the word for a bribe in the Far East), but, secondly and more importantly, because it wasn't enough! Mr E Sayer, who had signed on in London as Supernumerary, signed off the day before we left.

5   JAPAN

We sailed at 6.33am on Saturday, 12 November and again, to avoid contact with Kuomintang warships and 'planes, our route to Japan was via the Bashi Channel, between the Batan Islands and Formosa (Taiwan), rather than through the Formosa Strait, between Formosa and mainland China. And, also as before, a Union Jack was spread over No.3 hatch so that we could be clearly identified as a British ship.

The British and United States Governments did not recognize the Kuomintang blockade of Communist-held ports, but, due to the blockade, few ships ran the gauntlet to these ports. A notable exception was the New York based Isbrandtsen Line whose ships continued to call regularly at Shanghai and other Communist-held ports and, in their newspaper advertisements, the name SHANGHAI was always highlighted. On 29 September, the Isbrandtsen Line ships *Flying Clipper*, *Flying Independent* and *Flying Trader* were stopped by Kuomintang warships at the mouth of the Yangtze. The first two, bound for the States, were taken to Tinghai, the Kuomintang naval base in the Chusan archipelago south of Shanghai, but, after a protest by the US Government, were allowed to proceed. The *Flying Trader*, on her way to Shanghai, was warned not to enter the port, but she ignored the warning and proceeded to the port to discharge her cargo.

On 7 October, after two British ships were taken to Tinghai, the South China Morning Post likened the Kuomintang action to piracy and said, 'If the British Government sincerely desires its merchant ships to continue trading with Chinese coast ports it must be prepared to offer reasonable safeguards to those ships, their crews, and their cargoes.' The newspaper recognized, however, that as the Communists now controlled the coastline opposite Formosa, the blockade was weakening and the Navy's first job was the defence of Formosa itself. This too was the objective of the US 5th Fleet which patrolled the Formosa Strait.

Towards the end of October, the British vessels *Wosang, Tsinan, Inchmull* and *Louise Moller* discharged in Shanghai after being met by Royal Navy destroyers at the mouth of the Yangtze and escorted into Chinese Territorial Waters. The Isbrandtsen Line's *Flying Cloud* was there at the same time and, when she left the Yangtze, was fired upon by a Kuomintang warship and received damage to her hull.
When we were leaving the Bashi Channel, at noon on the 13th, there was

another typhoon, about seven hundred and fifty miles to the northeast and proceeding on a westerly course towards the mainland. But by noon on the 14th, when approximately thirty miles south of Okinawa, we were about three hundred miles northwest of it and saw nothing of its violence.

We docked in Kobe at 11.30am on Wednesday, 16 November and, on the 19th, Dr Moloney inoculated me against typhus. And, having discharged and loaded cargo, we left for the overnight run to Nagoya at 4.9pm on the 22nd. We docked there at 9.54am on the 23rd and, when a trader came on board with literature advertising his wares, I ordered a 21-piece Satsuma ware tea set and a 51-piece Sone ware dinner set which were delivered, beautifully packed in wooden boxes, the next day. Mr Rankin also bought china and, not trusting the trader, he opened his box to check that everything was there. What a mistake that was; it had been beautifully packed in straw and old newspapers and he broke a piece trying to get it all back! The larger of my boxes, on which I painted the words 'Handle with care', lies in my garage. And a few years ago, I smoothed out the old Japanese newspapers and gave them to the Department of Oriental Studies at Edinburgh University. Incidentally, the tea and dinner sets so pleased my mother that she kept them only on display in a glass-fronted cabinet. The tea set was used only once and that was when she was in hospital and my wife made the tea in her house! I now have both sets and the dinner set is now unique as stamped on the bottom of every piece are the words 'Made in Occupied Japan'.

We sailed at 3.3pm on the 24th and arrived in Yokohama at 6.54am on the 25th to discharge the remainder of our outward cargo. We also loaded metal pipes, cases of nails, pencils, tea and insulators, for Alexandria, and oak timber, for Antwerp. before sailing for Otaru, at 5.51pm the next day.

The weather and scenery were beautiful as we sailed, first along the east coast of northern Honshu and then through the Tsuguru Strait, between Honshu and Hokkaido, to Otaru, in Ishikari Bay, on the western side of Hokkaido. But, although it was still only November, it became quite cold as we headed north and there was snow on the mountains. On latitude 43°15′ North, Otaru is on almost the same latitude as Marseilles, but because Northern Honshu and Hokkaido lie on the eastern side of a continent, they have the same Laurentian climate as Eastern Canada and the North-East USA and experience the same cold winters.

We anchored off Otaru at 3.27pm on Monday, 28 November and, using our derricks, loaded undressed oak timber, consigned to Antwerp and

Alexandria, from barges. Afterwards, and purely as a matter of interest, I calculated the cost of shipping this and was surprised at the high figure arrived at. And as the timber was merely a 'drop in the bucket' in our voluminous holds, the freight charge on our total cargo must have been considerable indeed. Traders came out to the ship to offer us their wares and I bought a decorated wooden music box which played a lovely tune called 'China Night'.

6 THE HOMEWARD RUN BEGINS

We sailed for Hong Kong at 6.12am on Wednesday the 30th and, once we had again negotiated the Tsuguru Strait, were delighted to find that we were speeding along at 19 knots due to the influence of the Oyashio Current, travelling in the same direction. During the 5½-day run to Hong Kong, the *Glengarry* rolled badly in a heavy swell, an indication that there was a storm some distance away. As 1st Mate, Mr Letty was responsible for cargo stowage and seated in my cabin one day, he expressed anxiety at the way she was rolling.

We anchored in Hong Kong Harbour at 5pm on Monday, 5 December and I received a letter from my brother, Eric, telling of how he had sung Pablo The Dreamer, with a verse in doubtful Spanish, in a competition at the Palais. Although, he hadn't won, he received a great ovation and his letter contained the additional news that he had been offered a trial with the Harp; a Dundee football team in the Junior League. In offices at home, the high sloping desks, with their associated high stools, were giving way to low flat desks and chairs and Eric reported that this had happened where he worked.

Having spent three days loading cases of tea, drums of tea-seed and stillingia oil and bundles of canes, from lighters, we sailed at 4.33pm on the 8th and went straight out into bad weather. Gerry was on the 4 to 8 watch with Mr Letty and, when the latter told him to take a break, he came to my cabin for a chat. But when he divulged that Mr Letty had been drinking, I urged him to get right back to the bridge. It was a dirty night when only the dark outlines of islands could be made out and there was always a great deal of traffic in the area. Shortly after this, Mr Letty was reported to be ill. Mr Atkinson took over his duties and I don't recall seeing Mr Letty for the rest of the voyage.

We docked in Singapore, astern of the *President Monroe*, at 4.45pm on Monday, 12 December and, when she sailed a day or two later, there was music playing and streamers thrown from her decks. I was at my desk one afternoon, when I had a surprise visit from Midshipman Dugald McNab who was now on the *Idomenius*, which lay beside us and was on the Singapore/Australia run. "Our Mate says he knows you", Dugald announced, "and says to come over to see him". The 1st Mate was Hywel (Huw) Davies who had been 3rd Mate and a pal of mine on the *Samforth*. But, as I had never forgiven Huw for letting me down over the payment of laundry in Montevideo, I did not go. Huw died some time in the 1960s, when nearing promotion to Master, and I have always regretted my obstinacy in not accepting his invitation.

The Master of the *Idomenius* was the notorious 'Pinky' Johnston, so called because of his florid appearance. On one of our visits to the port, I saw him walking on the quay with Molly Prevost who was to become his wife and who, I believe, came to regret marrying him. Stories flew about the Company regarding 'Pinky' Johnston and I think it was Mr Broome who told me that he seen 'Pinky' wet himself when in a rage. In the Blue Funnel Association Newsletter of May, 1995, John Godden recounted that, when a midshipman on the *Idom* during 1950/51 and due to bullying by 'Pinky', he walked off from the wheel as the ship was entering Adelaide with a pilot on board. It was a courageous but rash action. Mr Godden, however, returned to the wheel and it seems that his misdemeanour was not reported.

We left Singapore at 5.3pm on the 17th and docked in Port Swettenham at 7.51am the following day. We sailed again at 3.42pm on the 20th, docked in Georgetown, Penang at 4.24am on the 21st and cleared the port at 12.15am on the 22nd.

7   CHRISTMAS 1949

It was a somewhat wild night when we arrived off Colombo at midnight on Christmas Eve and I leaned on the boat deck rail, enjoying the spectacle of the lighted town, as we were tossed about while waiting for the pilot to board. It was 1.30am before he had us tied up to buoys in the harbour and I remained up in case port officials appeared. None did, but, as Dr Moloney was ill, I was dug out of my bunk at 7am to receive the port doctor. When the Agent arrived shortly before breakfast, I received Christmas Cards and letters. And, welcome news for all of us, was that the self-insured Company was paying the annual Christmas bonus of one month's basic salary after a year of successful trading without mishap.

No loading was done that day, but it was a busy one for the Catering Department and the ship was in festive mood. We dressed in our No. 10's (white patrol jackets and long trousers) while the lady passengers wore evening dress and the men sported cummerbunds. Our passengers were Mr and Mrs Killick and their baby daughter (from Yokohama), Captain Donaldson, RN and his wife, four female German missionaries and one female Danish missionary (from Hong Kong), Mr and Mrs Clark and their children and Commander Wroughton, RN (from Singapore).

The evening's festivities began at 6pm with a punch party in the passengers' lounge thrown by Captain and Mrs Donaldson and Mr and Mrs Killick. The punch, made with milk, eggs and brandy, tasted excellent and the silver bowl was emptied before we descended to the saloon, hung with decorations, for dinner.

The menu card was a specially printed, folded, one and inside read as follows:

MENU

Grape Fruit Maraschino
Cocktail   Hors d'OEUVRE, Varies
Clear Turtle   Potage Marquise
Steamed Halibut, Mayonnaise
Calf's Sweetbreads with Champignon
Sirloin & Ribs of Beef, Hossoise, Yorkshire Fritters
Fresh Peas   Brussels Sprouts   Boiled Rice
Creamed, Straw & Boiled Potatoes

            Braised Turkey, Cranberry Sauce
             Baked Smoked Ham & Spinach
                   Salads in Season
          Plum Pudding, Brandy Sauce   Yule Log
                   Strawberry Ices
            Christmas Cake   Mince Pies
               Devilled Chicken Livers
                Dessert   Coffee
                    Cold Buffet
              Roast Lamb   Ox Tongue

We were all provided with paper hats, smiling stewards carried in flaming plum puddings, wine flowed and there was a big cigar for anyone who wanted one. I smoked mine and Dick found this amusing as, like him, I was a non-smoker.

Towards the end of the meal, a steward presented me with 'the Captain's compliments' and said that Captain MacTavish wanted to speak to me. And, when I went across to his table, Captain MacTavish said that we'd be going to the passengers' lounge to hear the King's (George VI) Christmas Day Message to the Commonwealth and asked me to tune it in on the radiogram. I said I would although I had never before used the set and didn't know the appropriate short-wave frequency. When I returned to my table and voiced my ignorance of the short-wave frequency, I think it was Gerry who said, "Won't Radio Ceylon broadcast the King's speech?" I hadn't thought of this, but believed that he was likely to be right so that I tuned into the local station. All, except the engineers and Dick, who was not given to parties and went to bed, repaired to the lounge upstairs and stood listening to the radio, but nobody else was aware of the relief I experienced when the National Anthem, heralding the King's Speech, was played! When the Speech ended, Captain MacTavish proposed the toast to the King.

The ritual over, we chatted to the passengers and Mr Rankin, Gerry and I returned their hospitality by providing them with drinks. Captain Donaldson was a tall, strong-looking, balding man, who appeared to be in his fifties. He had been the Naval Attaché to the British Embassy in Nanking during the *Amethyst* crisis and Lieut. Commander Kerans, who took command of the ship and brought her out of the Yangtze, had been his assistant. He was an easy man to talk to and, although Gerry and I spent a couple of hours in his company, the *Amethyst* was not mentioned.

I left the passengers' lounge to join the engineers who were conducting their own riotous celebrations in the smoke room. With their patrol jackets open and bottles strewn on tables and in buckets on the floor, they were bawling their heads off. I contributed by playing my mouth organ and remained for about an hour before heading for my bunk next door.

There were no docking facilities in Colombo. All ships lay within about half a mile of the Passenger Jetty and the return fare, by motor launch, was Rs2 (3/-/15p). Dick and I went ashore on Boxing Day and took a taxi to Mount Lavinia, seven miles to the south of the town. And as we made our way to seats on the terrace of the [3]Grand Hotel, which was busy due to a passenger ship being in port, we were just as surprised to see Captain MacTavish, in the company of some of our passengers, as he was to see us. It was a lovely day and very pleasant to sit on the terrace, by the beautiful beach and waving palm trees. On our way back to Colombo, we had the taxi driver take us to a Buddhist temple, but, when a horde of Buddhist monks, clad in their saffron coloured robes, approached the taxi, we hurriedly told the driver to drive on.

Although I had gone to sea in 1943, this was only my fourth Christmas outside the UK. In 1943, I had been in Oran on the *Samite* where, due to circumstances, the food was poor and there was no Christmas spirit. In 1944, I had been nearing Canada on the *Samforth* where the dinner was excellent, but the weather atrocious. Christmas 1946, spent on the *Samnesse* in Tanga, Tanganyika, had been good, but that Christmas on the *Glengarry* in Colombo was easily the best and I could not have enjoyed myself more if I had been at home. Christmas 1948, however, had not been spent at home, but with Marie and Stuart Crabb in Glasgow, when I was on the *Eurybates*, and I was destined to spend Christmas 1950 with them.

One man who didn't enjoy that Christmas was Dr Moloney as he had contracted pneumonia. Before we sailed from Colombo at 1.36pm on Wednesday, 28 December, I went ashore with Captain MacTavish to see to his paying off and was on the jetty to meet the launch which brought him from the ship. With his blue trench coat over his pyjamas, he made a sorrowful figure, but when I was helping him up the stone stairs from the launch, he said to me, "This is what I get for putting up the new calendar

---

[3] The 'rate per day per person inclusive' at the Grand Hotel was Rs17.50 to Rs21.00 (£1.31p to £1.57½p) and, at a later date, the Hotel and beach were used as a set in the film "The Bridge On The River Kwai".

before the Old Year is out!" Mr Atkinson had accompanied Dr Moloney in the launch and he and I went with him in the taxi which took him to the General Hospital, in a pleasant suburb, about three miles from the jetty and staffed by British nurses. And as this was my third trip with Dr Moloney and we had been good friends, I was sorry to leave him behind.

We loaded the usual tea in Colombo and some of us made private purchases at the kiosk of the Tea Propaganda Board on the passenger jetty. If tea were bought from any other source, it was not allowed to pass through Customs without an Export Coupon from the seller.

8   COLOMBO TO ADEN

After we had cleared Colombo, at 1.36pm on 28 December, with a complement of ninety-nine, I said to Captain MacTavish, "Do you know, sir, that if we had had one more person on board, we couldn't have sailed without a doctor?" "I am aware of that, Mr Malcolm," he replied.

If a crewmember sent a telegram from the ship, I debited the charge to his wage account. Passengers, however, paid in cash. This could be in any currency and when I passed the money over to Duncan, (which is how Dick and I referred to Captain MacTavish between ourselves) he always seemed to have a hard job sorting it out. It was of course desirable to keep the various currencies separate, but he went farther than that and stored coins of the same denomination in separate small tins. It was amusing to watch him operate his system.

The New Year of 1950 was heralded in when we were about a couple of days from Aden. Dick and I, who were teetotallers, went to bed as usual. But the off-duty engineers celebrated in the smoke room and, as this was next door to my cabin, I could hear the sound of their revelry into the small hours. On New Year's Day, I was very much surprised when King Tung Ling, our No.1 Bosun, came to my cabin with the present of a bottle of gin. While thanking him, I did my best to refuse it, but without success. A few days later, when I was in Captain MacTavish's cabin and he was pulling out every drawer looking for something, a similar bottle rolled to the front. "Now how did that get there?" he asked. I said nothing!

While the vessel was loading, the mates pencilled in the consignments on a cargo plan. Using indian ink, I had been making my fair copy since leaving Penang and, now that we had cleared Colombo, I completed it. It measured 15" by 39½", was headed as follows:

GLEN LINE LTD.
m.v. "GLENGARRY" VOY. 7 HOMEWARD
Sailed from (First Loading Port) KOBE on 22nd November, 1949
Sailed from (Last Loading Port) COLOMBO on 28th December, 1949
Draft Leaving Last Loading Port:- Forwd. 29'00" Aft. 31'00"
Fuel Oil Last Loading Port 690 tons

For:- Aden: Port Said: Alexandria: Genoa: London: Rotterdam: Hamburg: Antwerp.

The approximate tonnage distribution in tons of 20 cwt was entered into two printed boxes. One box showed the tonnage in the centre castle, 'tween deck, orlop deck and lower part of each hold. The other showed the tonnage for each port and the holds in which it was stowed.

The tonnage for the ports was as follows:

Aden - 124. Port Said - 83. Alexandria 577. Genoa - 370. London - 3352.
Rotterdam - 705. Hamburg - 1072. Antwerp - 1033. Copenhagen - 7 (To be discharged at Hamburg) Optional - 326. The total of 7649 tons was shown in both boxes mentioned above.

Most of the cargo from Malaya consisted of bales of rubber, but this didn't make the job any easier as each consignment had to be shown on the plan under its individual mark. Other cargo from Malaya was timber, rattans, copra, coconut oil in bulk, desiccated coconut, coco beans, apricot kernels, coffee, egg albumen, hides, bristles, chewing gum base (consigned to Wrigley), potassium iodide, sassafras oil, pineapples, soap, drums of latex, drums of wood oil, one Wolseley and one Austin car, pepper, plumbago, wolfram ore, lead, tin and 882 bags of mail.

When the plan, done on waxed paper, was completed, I made a copy of it by placing a sheet of light-sensitive beneath it in a glass frame and exposed it to the sun for a minute or so. Having already half-filled our bath, I then carried the blank sheet to the bath where I immersed it and the copy appeared. I had to make several copies then colour them and instructions on the original plan read:

HOMEWARD

Plans to be completed and forwarded from [4]Port Said by airmail as follows:

All Vessels 3 copies to Glen Line Limited, 20, Billiter Street, London,

---

[4] When I had previously done the job on the *Atreus*, I had understood that the plans (and cargo books) had to be sent from Aden and I always did this. It seemed to me that for vessels calling at Genoa or Marseilles, posting from Port Said to the Agents at these ports was cutting it rather fine.

E.C.3. who will distribute to N. Continental ports.
2 copies to Marine Superintendent, Glen Line, K.G.V. Dock, E.16.
1 copy to Alfred Holt & Company, India Buildings, Liverpool, 2.
Vessels calling at Genoa or Marseilles: 1 additional copy to Agents concerned.
Cargo for different ports to be shaded in different colours:-
LONDON - Red   HAMBURG - Blue   A/DAM. R/DAM. - Green
ANTWERP - Brown   GENOA - Yellow
When Fuel Oil is carried as cargo in D.B. Tanks and in consequence vessel has unfilled space in Holds through lack of draft state here the amount of such unfilled space, viz. tons of 40 cu. ft.
<u>Double Bottom Tanks</u>. Show whether empty or full (F.W., Oil Fuel, etc.) leaving last loading port.

I had also to type a cargo book to accompany each plan. These were composed from the information shown on the [5]boat notes which the 1st Mate signed when the cargo was loaded. First of all, I arranged them according to the port of discharge and then in alphabetical order according the consignment mark. When each book was typed, I stapled it between brown cardboard covers with the port of discharge shown on the front cover.

I believed the homeward system of cargo control to be efficient as, on receipt of the cargo plans and cargo books, marine superintendents at the various ports knew exactly what was coming and where it was in the ship. And labour and transport could be organised accordingly. The outward system, however, was another matter and I suspected that all the hard work that I had to put in, checking out the cargo, was more or less a waste of time. This view was later substantiated. By 1967, Holt ships carried only one radio officer/purser, and, to ease the increased workload, the outward system was entirely abolished. When containerisation was introduced, it simplified cargo handling, and today's 1st Mates have a much easier task regarding stowage and a ship's trim than their predecessors did on bulk-break ships.regarding stowage and a ship's trim than their predecessors did on bulk-break ships.

---

[5] This is what we called the 'mate's receipts' and the particulars on the bills of lading, the official receipts for goods shipped and signed by either the Master or the Agent, had to tally with those on the boat notes. There could be as many a 2000 bills of lading for our cargo, but the average number was 1200.

9   ADEN TO ALEXANDRIA

We anchored off Aden's Steamer Point at 3.15pm on Monday, 2 January, 1950 and having bunkered and discharged timber and cases of pineapples and soap into lighters, sailed again at 11.45pm. Dr J.W. Kendall, who had been left at Aden by the *Rhesus* (GRQJ), was brought out in the Agent's launch and I signed him on the Articles. Ships' surgeons had the name of being over-fond of alcohol, and, wearing his cap at a rakish angle, 46-year-old Dr Kendall was already in his cups. As his salary was only £35 a month, whereas Dr Moloney's had been £50, he couldn't have been long at sea, but he told me he had been to Antarctica.

Once my cargo plans and cargo books were handed to the Agent at Aden, the hard part of my job was over and I could relax. We anchored in Suez Bay at 4am on Friday, 6 January and, with a Canal pilot on board, left at 8.45am to negotiate the Canal in the daylight convoy. When we lay in the Bitter Lakes, waiting for the south bound convoy to appear, Captain MacTavish became impatient and, as we had 882 bags of mail for London on board, tried to jump the queue by claiming to the authorities that we were a Mail Ship. But they wouldn't accept this as their regulations defined mail ships as those 'performing a regular mail service under contract with a Government, at fixed dates appointed in advance' and we didn't qualify.

It was 11.39pm before we anchored in Port Said harbour and commenced discharging rattans and tapioca from Malaya and tea from Colombo. And, because I had to deal with the Agent, tally clerks and the Skipper, it was 1.30am before I got to bed. I was hauled out again at 4.30am when discharge was complete, but climbed back between the sheets as we left for Alexandria 4.57am.

The following extracts from our Agent's sailing sheet, dated 5 January, 1950, gives some idea of the British ships using the Canal at that time:

Wm. STAPLEDON & SONS

VESSELS EXPECTED AT SUEZ   HOMEWARD

BIBBY LINE
P Lancashire (H.T.) 27 Jan. U.K.
P Warwickshire   ear Feb. London, Liverpool.

BLUE FUNNEL LINE
 Mentor   6 Jan. Bilbao, Amsterdam, London, Liverpool.
X Antilochus   8 Jan.   Gibraltar, Tangier, Casablanca, Havre, Liverpool.
X Telemachus   9 Jan. Antwerp, Rotterdam, Hull, London.
 Talthybius   11 Jan. Odessa, Liverpool, Glasgow.
X [6]Herefordshire 16 Jan. Halifax, Boston, New York, Galveston, New Orleans.
 Tyndareus   20 Jan. Genoa, Marseilles, Dublin, Liverpool.

BROCKLEBANK LINE
X Macharda 10 Jan. Lisbon, Liverpool, Manchester, London, Boulogne, Dundee, Glasgow
X Marwarri   21 Jan. Casablanca, Lisbon, Glasgow, Dundee, London, Continent.
X Malakand   22 Jan. Boston, New York, Wilmington, Philadelphia, Baltimore, Norfolk.
X Mandasor   6 Feb. Barcelona, London, Dundee, Continent.
(Dundee was then the centre of the jute trade and Brocklebank ships brought the raw jute from Calcutta.)

CUNARD-WHITE STAR LINE
P Georgic   18 Mar. Rotterdam, Liverpool.

GLEN LINE
X Glengarry   6 Jan.   Alexandria, Genoa, London, Antwerp, Rotterdam, Hamburg.
X Radnorshire   22 Jan.   Tangier, Casablanca, Amsterdam, London, Hamburg.

N.S.M. "OCEAAN" (Dutch Blue Funnel)
Phrontis   10 Jan. London, Holland, Hamburg.

---

[6] (Not a Blue Funnel, but a Bibby Line ship.)

<u>ORIENT LINE</u>
P Orion   20 Jan.   Southampton.
P Ormonde   8 Jan.   London.
P Orcades   20 Feb.   London.

H.T. - HM Troopship   P - Passenger vessel   X - Limited passenger accommodation

We anchored in Alexandria harbour at 3.30pm the same day, Saturday, 7 January, 1950 and I met with Egyptian bureaucracy in the shape of four immigration officers plus their two assistants. Normally, I was asked for two copies of the crew lists which showed name, rank, age and nationality, but these guys demanded three, giving the additional information of where and when each man had signed on and Christian names. On top of this, all identity cards had to be presented for stamping in order to give us permission to land and, considering we were tied up to buoys in the harbour and leaving the next day, this was nonsense. In return for causing me all this trouble, the officials had to be given tea and cigarettes and obviously having nothing better to do, they remained on board for hours arguing about the merits of Islam and Christianity with our female missionary passengers. It was, however, a friendly discussion which both parties seemed to enjoy. We discharged the metal pipes, insulators, pencils and nails, from Yokohama, and the, mainly oak, timber, from Otaru. And as soon as this was out of the ship, sailed for Genoa at 2.30pm on the 8th.

10   GENOA AND HOME

It was a pleasure to make that beautiful passage between Sicily and the toe of Italy again. As the weather was superb, we could see Etna in the distance, to port, and, shortly after leaving the Strait, Stromboli, to starboard.

MacTavish rushed to clear Alexandria in order to reach Genoa by the evening of Wednesday, 11 January. All the mates believed this impossible and, when MacTavish realized that this was indeed the case, he reduced speed to 12½ knots on the 10th to arrive on Thursday morning. I had received letters from my parents and Eric at Suez and Port Said and, as I began my reply on Wednesday evening, the island of Monte Cristo was just visible in the gathering dusk. My father had reported that my Christmas cards had arrived on time and, in reply to his query as to how my studies and photography were coming along, I said pressure of work allowed no time. He and my mother had booked a tour of Italy and I offered to pay their return fare to Dover. I had asked Mother to buy a pair of blankets on my behalf and give them to my grandfather for Christmas and she had done so. In his letter, Eric had written that he had had a dance with Helen, my former girlfriend, at the Palais when she was home on leave. My name hadn't been mentioned, but I noted the fact that he believed she had no attachments!

When we docked in Genoa at 8.30am on Thursday, 12 January, the Customs gave me a hard time of it by requiring me to complete a form which asked for the weight of each item of cargo we had for Genoa. I could give them the total weight and the number of cases, etc., but had no idea of what was asked for. And, when I sat in the saloon, hot under the collar, trying to work this out, the officials sat about chatting. As when I had trouble on the *Atreus* with the Suez Canal form, nobody actually seemed to care and the figures I concocted were accepted without comment.

Captain MacTavish had Dr Kendall and me accompany him ashore to sign a deposition 'noting protest'. I quote from 'Ship's Business' by Bonwick and Steer: 'This is the procedure whereby a master makes a deposition before a notary public, Consul or magistrate, giving particulars of anything untoward which has occurred on the voyage and of any emergency measures which the master has taken. If, for example, bad weather has been experienced, the master should note protest in case damage has been done to ship and/or cargo of which he may or may not be aware.......The sworn testimony of the master and others should be borne out by production of, and entries in, the log book.......'. The three of us were taken by car to the court where we signed a deposition stating that the *Glengarry* had encountered bad weather in the China Sea and the Indian Ocean. Afterwards, when I pointed out to MacTavish that Dr Kendall had joined the ship only in Aden, he said he was aware of it. Although the port was a prosperous one, we encountered many poor looking souls as we walked back through the narrow streets of old town. And the black-market cigarette sellers were still there; people of all ages calling out "Cigarettes - Inglis - Americani". When I had my radio tuned in to the local station that evening, I heard the *Glengarry* mentioned and, as a strong wind had sprung up, it was a good night to be in port.

We had bales of rubber, bags of gum, drums of wood oil and ingots of tin to discharge. And, in the late evening, when I was already in bed, Dick came to me with a problem concerning the latter. Tin ingots are heavy and valuable. We had 1105 of them and Mr Atkinson, acting 1st Mate due to Mr Letty's incapacity, had come to him, when he too was in bed, to order him to tally their discharge. Dick was angry at this; not because he objected to doing the job, but because Atkinson had told him so late. I suggested to Dick that if he were called before 2am, he should do the job; otherwise refuse. Dick accepted the suggestion and, when he was called, by another mate, at about 3am, he refused to get up. Both of us, but particularly Dick, expected all hell to break loose the next day, but nothing more was heard! Anyway, Atkinson should have consulted me first and Dick and I stood together on everything. Incidentally, when we were in Tangier during the following voyage, the steward came into my cabin, when I was still in bed at 8am, with the message that the Captain wanted to see me. But when I told Captain MacTavish that I had been working all night and got to bed about 6am, he said, "I'm sorry, Mr. Malcolm, I didn't know."

Mr Atkinson, however, was not a bad bloke and we generally got on fine. I sat beside him at the meal table and once when the discussion had turned to railways and he asked a question, Dick, a mine of information on all things technical, launched into a mini-lecture. And after he had described Brunel's 7" gauge, used on the London - Bristol section of our railways, and how the 4′ 8" gauge, used throughout the rest of the UK, was chosen only because it was used by the first, coal mine, railways, Atkinson turned to me and said "I only *asked*."! A male passenger at our table continually complained about the mildness of the curries so that after he left one evening, Atkinson said, "For God's sake throw in more matches."!

We sailed from Genoa at 4.45pm on Friday, 13 January and, in spite of the superstitious date, enjoyed beautiful weather in the Mediterranean so that I saw the Balearic Islands, then devoid of package-holiday makers, in the distance.

At 1.45pm on 16 January, when we were in the Bay of Biscay, Dick took the following message from the outward bound *Telemachus* (GBLB): To PURSER GLENGARRY = PLEASE INFORM WHETHER INCOME TAX PAID ON XMAS BONUS IS NORMAL DEDUCTION = MARTIN. I answered in the affirmative.

Two days later, at 2.30pm on Wednesday, 18 January, and only five days after leaving Genoa, we picked up the Channel pilot at Brixham. It was again the time of excitement and packing and, by 3pm the next day, we passed through the locks and tied up in KGV at 4pm. And one of those waiting on the quay was Lieut. Comm. [7]Kerans, of HMS *Amethyst*, who had come to meet Captain Donaldson. No time was wasted. We paid off in the saloon about an hour later and, also in the saloon, a Customs Officer sat at a table, dealing with each of us in turn.

Prior to arriving home, we listed all the items we had to declare on a manifest. I had declared everything and the item on which I anticipated paying the most duty was a pair of binoculars bought in Japan. But, with the manifest before him, the Customs Officer did not even mention the binoculars and I paid duty only on the other articles declared. On returning to my cabin, however, I found that I had one pair of ladies' nylon stockings more than I had declared. And, not because I was so honest, but because Customs Searchers were still searching cabins, I went back to declare the additional pair of nylons to the Officer in the saloon. "Oh," he said, "I'm glad you came back. I forgot to ask about these binoculars." And I could have kicked myself for omitting the pair of nylons. "Where did you buy them? he asked, "Was it Aden?" He was putting words into my mouth. Aden was a British colony and less duty was paid on articles purchased in Colonies. I knew what he was doing, but as the binoculars had Tokyo emblazoned on them, I thought it wiser to admit that I had bought them in Japan. He then asked, "Are they new?" and I somewhat hedged by saying that I had been using them during the voyage. "Oh

---

[7] From 1960 to 1964, J.C. Kerans was Conservative Member of Parliament for The Hartlepools.

well," he said, "Because I forgot about them and have already put them down as second-hand, we'll let it go at that." The Customs Officers were decent if you were (relatively) honest with them.

My pink Customs slip read as follows:

ARTICLES FOR DUTY and/or PURCHASE TAX	Value	Duty+Purchase
	£ s. d.	£ s. d.
Three pairs a/s (artificial silk) Hose	15 0	15 0
One a/s article appl (real silk dressing gown)	7 0	4 8
One Linen (embroidered) Tablecloth	12 0	8 0
[8]One Wooden Article Furniture	2 0 0	13 4
	TOTAL	1 16 0 (£1.80p)

My relief, who was doing the coasting trip to the continental ports, came on board and, when he was talking to Dick and me and we were somewhat decrying the job at sea, he expressed the opposite view. In his forties, he had spent the war as a lieutenant in the Royal Navy; presumably on T124 or T124X articles which merchant seamen signed when their ship was requisitioned by the Navy. But, at that time, we regarded any sea-going R/O of such an advanced age as a dead-beat!

Dick, who lived in Chelsea, went home that evening, but it was the next day, Friday, 20 January, before I 'phoned Confair Radio Cabs, in Plaistow, to have them take me and my gear up to Euston Railway Station. It was a fairly long journey and taxis could be expensive, but, being on a regular run, we had learned that Confair's prices were reasonable so that we used this company regularly. To get out of the dock gate without the annoyance of having the PLA policeman search through my luggage, to check that I had no more dutiable goods than those listed on my pink customs slip, I placed the required half-crown (12½p) inside the folded slip and gave it to the driver. He handed it to the policeman and, after a slow walk to his hut, he returned the slip, minus the half-crown, to the driver. This was the

---

[8] This was a camphor wood chest which I took through Customs for Gerry Davies, but Gerry left the ship without reimbursing me.

normal despicable practice of the Port of London Authority Police which I had first experienced when the *Samite* docked during the war.

I went to Euston because I was heading for Glasgow, and not Dundee, as I had arranged to spend the weekend with Marie. I travelled on the night train and arrived in Glasgow shortly after 6am the next day. We went to the Plaza Ballroom that evening and on Monday morning I travelled through to Dundee. And when the train arrived in the West Station at 12.32pm, I found that my father waiting on the platform.

While on leave, I typed the following letter and sent it to Dick to add his signature:

3rd February, 1950

Steamship Department,
Messrs Alfred Holt & Co.,
Liverpool 2.

Dear Sirs,
    During the recent voyage of the "Glengarry", Capt. MacTavish has requested the daily presentation of a news-sheet; this being his interpretation of a Company Circular issued to Masters some time ago. The news-sheet is for the benefit of the passengers.
    We feel that, as there is a Reece-Mace radiogram in the passengers' lounge, the composition of such a news-sheet only means considerable unnecessary work during 'off watch' periods.
    At the same time, however, we realise that conditions for reception may, on occasions, be unsuitable and, on such occasions, we should only be too pleased to co-operate by publishing a news-sheet. By experience, however, we know such occasions to be rare, as private receivers throughout the ship obtain clear reception each evening if not during the daylight hours. B.B.C. news broadcasts are relayed on shortwave by Radios Ceylon, Singapore and Australia, thus enabling us to listen to 'Home' news with a minimum of effort.
    We respectfully suggest, therefore, that a notice be circularised to the effect that a news-sheet is necessary only when conditions for reception are poor and pointing out that a daily news-sheet means only additional unnecessary work to the radio officer during his 'off duty' periods.
    Please do not regard this letter as a complaint against the instructions of Capt. MacTavish as we have obtained his permission to ask for clarification of the matter.

As there was no telephone in my house, Calverley 'phoned Dick to say that Duncan was quite wrong and that he would sort out the matter. The news-sheet was, therefore, abandoned, but I placated Duncan by offering him an abbreviated one for his personal use. Unlike most of us, he didn't have a personal radio and the compromise delighted him.

11   REJOINING AGAIN

When I returned to the ship after over three weeks leave, Chu Ching Fah, our 22-year-old cabin steward, spotted the arrival of my taxi and hastened down from the boat deck to take possession of my cabin trunk. It was a heavy trunk and, although he was a slightly built lad, he scorned my attempt to help him with it, and carried it on his shoulder up the steep gangway and then up to my room, two decks above.

Chu, who had rather long lank jet-black hair, was, due to his behaviour, rather unkindly referred to by Dick and me as 'The Genius'. One day, when he had been given the job of summoning the deck officers and passengers to dinner by striking the xylophone, Dick saw him standing, with the instrument in his hands and his eyes on the saloon clock. As the bewitching hour approached, the suspense became too much for Chu and, with about a minute to go, he pushed the hand to the hour and strode off knocking hell out of the xylophone which was already falling apart and held together by pieces of string. Incidentally, the off-watch engineer officers were summoned by a steward banging on a gong. Some of them took the opportunity to have a nap before dinner and presumably the more dulcet tones of the xylophone had sometimes failed to waken them!

Chu did not normally serve in the saloon, but one morning when he was promoted to serve breakfast, his almost total lack of English put him under great pressure. When we asked for grapefruit, he brought cornflakes and when we said it was grapefruit we wanted, he returned with shredded wheat. I don't think he was asked to do the job again, but I'm sure we would have done no better if the ordering had been done in Chinese.

Towards the end of the voyage on which we were about to embark, Dick and I decided that it would be useful to have a bookshelf fitted to the bulkhead above the desk in the wireless room. To mark out in chalk exactly where we wanted the shelf, we climbed up on the desk. This brought us near to the brass clock, which was kept shining by Chu, and it was only then that we saw that the left-hand side of the clock, which could not be seen from the floor, was a dull green due to never having been touched!

Chu was the youngest and least experienced of the seven Assistant Stewards and Chen Ling Yueh, aged 43, said proudly to me "Me one-time Blue Funna Li (Blue Funnel Line)" and "One-time (the prestigious)

Shanghai Club." In addition to the seven, all of whom were friendly, Taey Teh Yuen, aged 48, was the Captain's Steward/'Tiger' and Chu Ching Foo, aged 34, was Head Waiter.

All officers and passengers were wakened by a steward bringing them a mug of tea, and tea and toast was served in the afternoon. Sunday was recognized as a special day by buns, known as tabnabs, being served instead of toast. I was on day shift on all the ships I served on after the war and I always told the steward not to bring me morning tea. This allowed me another half-hour in bed and it was ghastly stuff anyway, over sweetened by evaporated milk.

As many of the Chinese could neither read nor write, they signed the Articles by making their mark. This might be a simple cross, but I have seen men laboriously drawing shapes with an intensity of concentration which showed that they were unused to holding a pen. Their fingerprints also went on the Articles and, when I was engaged in signing them on, I pressed their thumbs on an inkpad and then on the paper. But, whatever their standard of formal education, the Chinese were capable in all departments and kept the ship in tiptop condition. It was left to them to acquire sufficient English in order to do what was required of them. I never came across one British officer who knew any Chinese.

As my cabin was in such an isolated position at the after end of the boat deck, I used to think that I was vulnerable if the Chinese were to make trouble. There was one particular seaman who caught my attention. He was a strong-looking stocky man who looked decidedly vicious and I thought that I wouldn't like to come across him on a dark night. But once, when I was going ashore in Hong Kong in a sampan crewed by women, I had a job preventing this smiling friendly fellow from paying my fare! I wish now that I had taken the trouble to learn something of their language.

I had got to know David Logan during my spell at Leith Nautical College. At that time he had worked in the Scotsman offices at North Bridge, in Edinburgh, but, as he had since been transferred to their Fleet Street office, shared by the Evening Standard, I 'phoned to arrange a meeting.

Friday, 17 February, 1950 was the Chinese New Year, but there were no signs of revelry among the crew when David spent the evening on board the ship. The next day, I met him in Trafalgar Square at 3.30pm and, after going to a cinema and having tea in the City, we went to a hospital dance in Plaistow. I knew of the dance because the relieving 2nd Mate had gone up to the hospital with toothache and, when it was learned that he was from a ship, he had been told to come along and to bring shipmates. The nurses made us welcome, there was lots to eat and a crowd of us returned to the ship by taxi with David in the middle. In order to be admitted into the docks, you had to have a pass. But, on this occasion, I didn't have one for David and, when the policeman asked, "What ship?" we all shouted "Glengarry" and he waved us on. David slept on my settee that night and had breakfast before leaving the ship.

When we were in London or Liverpool, we had to sign for our meals as all sorts of port people ate in the saloon. But, before I could tell David not to sign the book, he had already signed and nothing came of it. There was a story going about at the time that Holts were so concerned about the number of men eating on board their ships that they began to examine the books carefully. You had to put your occupation beside your signature and, on examining one book, they came across the same signature, appearing time and time again, with the occupation given as C/D. This puzzled them so that they followed it up to discover the C/D stood for crane driver! We all laughed about this, but, if the story were true, that crane driver must have had a brass neck indeed.

Dick and I were asked to join Holt's own Superannuation Scheme and arrangements were made for us to be examined by doctors at the head London office of the London & Liverpool & Globe Insurance Company, at 1 Cornhill, who ran the Scheme. We went there together, but saw different doctors. Dick was examined by Sir Somebody or Other and the one who examined me was a former Lieut. Colonel who talked about the forthcoming General Election. Having both passed the medical, we were admitted into the Scheme and, from 1 March, 1950, contributed to it instead of to the Merchant Navy Officers' Pension Fund (MNOPF).

The Articles, opened by Captain W.F. Dark, were signed in the saloon on Tuesday, 21 February. I was in Captain MacTavish's cabin that evening when a greaser, who was refusing to sail, was brought in by Mr Topley, the Chief Engineer, and another Chinaman of the engine room staff. Holts had a Chinese interpreter, but, as he was not present, it was found impossible to ascertain why the man was refusing to sail. MacTavish tried to persuade him, but the man, who was obviously distraught, remained adamant. He was taken ashore in the morning and a replacement was signed on. Strangely enough, on Form Eng.2 'ACCOUNT of CHANGES in the CREW of a FOREIGN-GOING SHIP' the name of the man who left the ship and that of the one who joined, were both given as Yu Chang Kan.

The rate of pay of a Chinese greaser was £12.3.6d a month at a time when a British greaser would have received nearer £20. Similar to the lascars/Indian seamen who were employed by other companies, such as Brocklebank, the Chinese were cheap and the equivalent of today's Filipinos.

Holts supplied each of us with an airmail postings list so that we could advise our correspondents as to the latest dates for posting directly to us, care of the Agents, at our various ports of call. Up to given dates they could write to the ship c/o William Stapledon & Sons, Port Said, The Halal Shipping Co. Ltd., Aden, Boustead & Co. Ltd., Penang and Singapore, Jardine, Matheson & Co. Ltd., Hong Kong and Kobe, Whittal & Co., Colombo and, if calling, M.H. Bland & Co. Ltd., Tangier and Anglo-Moroccan Shipping Agency, Casablanca. This was the first time I had experienced this facility and it greatly speeded up the delivery of mail which would otherwise have been sent either to Holt's office in Liverpool or to the Glen Line office in London for onward transmission to us.

The airmail postage rates shown on the sheet were: Aden, Egypt, Morocco - 6d per ½ oz. Ceylon, Malaya, Hong Kong - 1/- per ½ oz. Japan - 1/3d per ½ oz. Alternatively, Air Letter forms could be sent for 6d to all destinations.

12   SHIPMATES

Captain MacTavish remained as Master, but all the mates had been changed.

The 1st Mate was R.T. Horan, aged 35, who had commanded the corvette HMS *Bergamot* in Russian convoys during the war and had emerged as a Lieut. Commander, RNR with a DSC, Mentioned in Dispatches and the USSR's Order of the Red Star. One of those hard-working men, determined to succeed, he became a Marine Superintendent, but died in his early forties.

The 2nd Mate was D.H. Stewart, a fresh-faced heavily built jovial man from Lifford in County Donegal, who, with his sparse hair, looked older than his 29 years. I sat beside him at his table in the saloon where I soon learned that 'bovine' was a favourite word of his as he was forever using that adjective to describe people. Desmond had been on the *Cyclops* when she had been torpedoed 125 miles southeast of Cape Sable, Nova Scotia, in 1942 and, for his bravery, had been awarded Lloyds' War Medal and a Commendation in the London Gazette. Later that same year, he was on the *Glenorchy* when she was sunk, while carrying drums of aviation spirit, in the most famous of the Malta convoys - 'Pedestal'. Of the fourteen ships in the convoy, only five, including the battered tanker *Ohio*, reached Malta. Desmond was in one of the two [9]lifeboats which landed in Tunisia where the men were interned until the Allies landed in western North Africa in November. He then joined the RNR and, shortly before he retired as Master, in 1976, was awarded the CBE for service in the RNR in which he had attained the rank of Commodore.

The 3rd Mate was 22-year-old P.N. (Nick) Broad, a tall man from Bexhill in Sussex.

The Extra 3rd Mate, Tao Chi Yuan, was 23 and Chinese, and the only non-British officer I ever sailed with. His hometown was Wusih, in Kiangsu Province, about 100 miles northwest of Shanghai, and, because he signed the European Articles, I put him on the European Crew List where I showed his name as C.Y. Tao. As Chi had a limited command of English,

---

[9] Captain R.A. Hanney, with whom I had been on the *Eurybates*, was Mate of the *Glenorchy*. His lifeboat was captured by an Italian M.A.S. (M.T.B.) and its occupants taken to Italy where they remained prisoners until Italy surrendered in September, 1943.

it was difficult to have a conversation with him. Nevertheless, he had a British 2nd Mate's Certificate, as did Mr Broad. The 1st and 2nd Mates had their Masters'.

We had previously carried only two midshipmen, but now we had four: C.M. Sandy, the senior and a son of the manse from Whitstable in Kent, P.A.I. Latham, from Tomatin in Invernessshire, T.L. Murdoch from Holywood, County Down, and H.C. Kershaw from Birkenhead. The latter was aged 16 and the others 18. Mr Sandy became a Master.

The Engineers were mostly the same, but N. Reid, who had his 1st Class Motor Certificate, had replaced *W.J. Edwards as 2nd and H. Cowling and J.E. Kingham, both aged 22, had replaced R. Boardman and J.K. Oldman as uncertificated Assistant Engineers. Mr Kingham became an Engineer Marine Superintendent with another shipping line while Mr Kenworthy, who was still with us as an Assistant Engineer, became a Chief Engineer in the Company.

J.R. Forret, aged 21, had replaced C.V. Green as 2nd Electrician and R. Gray, also aged 21, had replaced [10]W.T. Lawless as 2nd Steward.

J.B. Taylor, a 26-year-old newly qualified doctor on his first voyage, was Surgeon.

C. Smith, aged 53, was Carpenter and 23-year-old R. Silsby, who was signed on as a Supernumerary Carpenter's Mate at a pay of £25 a month, was going out to join the *Patroclus*.

The 1st, 2nd, 3rd and Extra 3rd Mates were paid £54, £48, £37 and £37 respectively. The Chief, 2nd and 3rd Engineers, all of whom were certificated, were paid £68, £52 and £43 respectively and the uncertificated Refrigeration Engineer, £40. The uncertificated 4th Engineer - £33. Assistant Engineers Cowling and Kingham - £31. Other Assistants - £30. 1st and 2nd Electricians - £40 and £36. Chief and 2nd Stewards - £42-10/- and £29. Surgeon - £35. Carpenter - £39-5/-. I was still on £38, plus £6 Purser's Bonus, and my basic pay would be increased when I completed my seventh year at sea, in July. Dick was still on £28-10/-.

In addition to the pukka wages book, I kept a rough one showing the daily

---

[10] These men had both been on the previous three voyages.

amount each man left himself to spend, and which bore no relation to his salary. The allotment was the biggest deduction and leaving £22 a month, to be banked for me by my mother, I was left with 5/4d (26½p). Dick, who allotted £10 monthly, was left with 8/6d (42½p) and Dr Taylor, who made no allotment, 19/10d (99p); more than anyone else on board. Dr Taylor was the exception; even the midshipmen, on meagre salaries, left allotments. Mr Sandy, allotting £4-15/- (£4.75p), left himself a daily spending sum of 3/2d (16p) while Messrs Murdoch and Latham, allotting £4-10/- (£4.50p), were each left with 3/- (15p). Mr Kershaw, who would appear to be paid less because he was under 18, left £3-13/- (£3.65p) so that 2/5d (12p) remained for him to spend. I have commented on Mr Kershaw's salary because he was paid less than Mr Latham who was a 'first tripper'. All the midshipmen, except the latter, joined the ship with credit balances of £13, £25 and £2 respectively, shown in their books.

Besides our other passengers, we had two who signed on as Supernumeraries at the nominal pay of 1/- (5p) a month and were embarking, courtesy of the Company, on a long holiday, to the Far East and Australia. These were Mrs C. Savery, aged 49, and Miss E.K. Savery, aged 21, who were the wife and daughter of Captain P.W. Savery, the Master of another Glen Line ship on the same run. They were to be with us until our return to Singapore on the homeward run when they would transfer to a Blue Funnel ship on the Singapore/Australia service. This was Elsa's first voyage, but her mother had travelled on the *Protesilaus* in 1936. Someone told me that when Captain Savery had been asked why he had not had his wife and daughter travel with him, he had expressed abhorrence at the idea!

13 VOYAGE 8 OF THE GLENGARRY BEGINS

Shortly after leaving King George V Dock at Silvertown, at 2pm on Wednesday, 22 February, 1950, Dick sent our usual [11]TR to Northforelandradio (GNF) GNF de GNCS (our call sign) - 'GLENGARRY QTO (leaving) LONDON BOUND FAR EAST QSX (listening) AREA 1A'. (Messages to ships in Areas 1A and 1B, extending to the Southern Red Sea, were broadcast by Portisheadradio, at Highbridge in Somerset, and GNF would inform them, by teleprinter, that we were listening to their broadcasts.

Before the above message could be transmitted, however, a new main aerial had to be put up. And, as the long aerial, with insulators at each end, had to be slung between the masts, the bosun and several of the crew were engaged in the work which Dick and I supervised. The aerial had to be passed round the outside of the rigging and when the triatic stay, running from the after end of the funnel to the main mast, got in the way, Dick decided that it could be removed. This was not only because it was proving an obstruction, but also because it was never used and the aerial down-lead could short against it when we were transmitting. But before the Bosun complied with our instruction, he gestured to show that he thought the stay supported the funnel which might fall down without it!

This work was in progress as we passed through the lock gate into the Thames and, as the gate was part of Manor Way, there were buses and cars held up at each side, waiting for it to be closed behind us. The people were, of course, all looking at the big ship as she moved slowly past and I felt happy and glad that my life was more adventurous and interesting than most of theirs.

Holts were generally slow in adopting new practices, but, during the ship's stay in London, a radar room had been built on, aft of the chart room, and the device, at last, reinstalled. And I say reinstalled because she had it when sailing under the German flag as the "Hansa" during the war.

Although the Master retained overall command, the Trinity House pilots had the responsibility of navigating the ship in the Thames/Channel area. A River Thames pilot took the ship from KGV to Gravesend. At Gravesend, the River pilot landed and a Channel pilot boarded. If he were

---

[11] The name given to this type of message.

not also a Deep Sea pilot, the Channel pilot disembarked to the Dungeness cruising pilot cutter, otherwise he continued to Brixham. The reverse sequence applied on the inward journey. Under the Pilotage Act of 1913, the berth to Dungeness passage was compulsory, but the Dungeness to Brixham passage was not. And Trinity House informs me that it is likely that Glen Line used choice pilots, i.e. those retained by the Company, and not ordinarily rostered pilots.

The General Election, already referred to, was held on Thursday, 23 February and, before we left London, I heard Captain MacTavish talking about the Covenanters. He was not, however, referring to those who had signed the National Covenant of 1643 as, at what was described as a non-political Scottish National Assembly, held in Edinburgh on 29 October, 1949, a second National Covenant had been launched, binding the signatories to work for the establishment of a Scottish Parliament to control internal affairs. By the time of the General Election, a million people had signed, but it 6 May, 1999 before their aim was achieved.

Labour, who had been elected by a landslide in 1945, was returned, but with such a narrow and unworkable majority, of five, that another Election, which the Conservatives won, was held the following year. I believe Captain MacTavish's constituency was Kelvingrove where Walter Elliot, the Conservative candidate, was elected with 15,197 votes. Standing against him, C.M.Grieve, the Scottish National Party candidate, received only 639 votes. Christopher Grieve, the renowned Scottish poet who wrote under the name Hugh McDiarmid, was a Communist and one of the founders of the SNP. And it is interesting to compare his poor showing with the support which the Nationalists receive today. In that same election, Willie Gallacher, the Communist MP for West Fife, lost his seat to Willie Hamilton, the Labour candidate. Although aged 24, this was the first time I was eligible to vote in a General Election and my father cast my vote by proxy. The voting age was 21 and I had been only 20 at the time of the 1945 General Election.

I do not recall if Dick heard the SOS, but, when we were in the Bay of Biscay, on Friday, 24 February, fire broke out on the *Benledi* (Captain J Liston) when she was 160 east of Malta, bound for the Far East, and she became a total loss. The fire, which started in the stokehold, burst the oil tanks. The crew, who had taken to the lifeboats, were picked up by the tanker *British Liberty* then transferred to the destroyer HMS *Childers* which took them to Malta.

As regards the triatic stay, it did not take Horan long to see that it had been removed. He had it restored and justifiably complained that we had no right to alter any part of the ship's structure without his permission. But, shortly after we passed Gibraltar, Horan was standing on the boat deck beside us watching the homeward bound *Glenearn*, of similar design, pass us. "Look," said Dick, "She doesn't have the stay." Horan made no comment: he was unable to give any reason for retaining the stay other than that it was shown on the rigging plan.

I quote from a letter I received from Dick many years ago, in which he suggests a reason as to why the *Glengarry* had the triatic stay and the *Glenearn* didn't. "The *Glenearn* had the old fashioned engine room ventilators which were turned to face the wind and therefore did not rely on any sort of power. The *Glengarry*, on the other hand, had forced ventilation by means of four large fans, one at each corner of the engine room casing. So, if the fans failed for any reason, the engine room would not have any ventilation. In that case, wind stockings could be suspended from the triatic stay and fed through the engine room skylight...... And yet, looking back, I don't remember seeing any pulley blocks or halyards on the triatic stay, so it would have to be lowered for those to be fitted. So why not leave it lowered until some emergency arose?"

Incidentally, Dr Taylor, who had not yet got his 'sea legs', was confined to his bunk during the passage through the Bay of Biscay.

14   PORT SAID TO MALAYA

Port Said was reached at 4.30pm on Thursday, 2 March and the familiar procedure ensued. A British pilot took us in, an Egyptian doctor boarded and, as soon as he had Dr Taylor sign that there was no infectious disease on board, the quarantine flag came down and the bumboat men stormed on board with their wares. The Agent brought mail and, according to Dick, for I have no recollection of the matter, he asked me for the deadweight tonnage of the ship. I knew the gross and net tonnages (9838 and 5863) by heart, but had never before been asked for the deadweight which is the difference between a ship's displacement at load and light drafts and the measure of her capacity to carry cargo, fuel, passengers and crew. Somehow or other, Dick and I came up with the figure of 18000 tons. The Agent accepted the figure and we heard no more about it. But why he required the deadweight tonnage remains a mystery to me as Suez Canal dues were based on a gross and net tonnage arrived at by their own system of measurement. They did not accept national tonnage certificates.

As we had cargo for Port Said, it was 1.36pm the next day before, with a Canal pilot on board, we weighed anchor and entered the Canal in convoy. In order to reduce erosion of the Canal banks by a ship's wash, the maximum permitted speed was 7½ knots and, when transit was made at night, ships were required to have a projector/searchlight at their bows, capable of illuminating the Canal 1200 metres ahead. The Canal Company hired out projectors, but all Holt vessels, using the Canal regularly, had their own. If the Canal authorities wished to contact the pilot, they did this by hoisting either flags, or lights, at a Canal station such as Ismailia. If the pilot wished to contact the authorities, we were at his disposal and could communicate with their radio station (SUQ). We transmitted on 425 kcs and they replied on 400 kcs (now khz). We did not keep a radio watch in the Canal, but left our receiver on the latter frequency throughout the passage. We exited into Suez Bay at 5.54am on Saturday, 4 March and, having disembarked the pilot, it was 'full away' for Aden.

The timetable of the *Glengarry* and the other eight fast Glen [12]boats, all averaging over seventeen knots, was very regular: London to Gibraltar -

---

[12] Sailors do not generally like their ships being referred to as 'boats', but we spoke of Glen boats, Sam boats (the British Liberty ships with the prefix SAM) and banana boats. Some even referred to the latter ships, owned by Elders and Fyffes Ltd., as the 'skin' boats!

three days; Gibraltar to Port Said - five; Suez to Aden - three; Aden to Penang - eight. With the days spent in Port Said, the Canal and Aden added to these nineteen, it was twenty-two days from London to Penang. The old *Atreus* and the other ships of her generation, averaging over eleven knots and sailing from Birkenhead, took twenty-eight days to Penang. All on the *Glengarry* were proud of her speed, but, as it drastically reduced the time at sea and therefore that available to do my work, it increased the pressure and was a mixed blessing. On the positive side, of course, I had a comfortable cabin with a large desk, instead of the mere plank, hooked onto my bunk, as I did on the *Atreus*; plus an office, cooling blowers throughout the ship and a modern radio room with a short-wave transmitter. There was just no comparison between the ships and even although the *Glengarry* went as far the Japanese ports, when the *Atreus*, during my voyage on her, went only as far as Hong Kong, the round trip was faster.

I have already mentioned that I was responsible for the issuing of shore passes. These included passes to permit our Chinese to take articles ashore and was an absolute chore when the pressure of work was on me in port. With the benefit of experience, therefore, I got Dick, who, like myself, could touch-type, to type several blank passes requiring only the details to be inserted at the time of issue. The passes read: 'Please pass bearer (name) with (description of article which could be 'One dried fish'!) .... Signed D MacTavish, Master. Captain MacTavish never saw the passes; his rubber-stamp signature being applied, as it also was on the crew lists.

We arrived in Penang at noon on Thursday, 16 March and my hectic work, previously described, began. We left Penang at 3.12pm on the 17th, arrived at Port Swettenham at 7.51am on the 18th and left at 7.24pm on the 19th.

On the way to Singapore, Dr Taylor inoculated me against cholera and we docked at the West Wharf, not far from the *Orestes* and *Aeneas*, at 5.31pm on Monday the 20th. Midshipman Colin Sandy left the ship for transferral to the *Eurybates* while 20-year-old M Collyer, from that ship, signed on as Supernumerary 4th Mate.
When working at my desk one afternoon, Captain MacTavish, accompanied by a lady who was not a passenger, came to ask if I knew if it were possible to 'phone home. Normally, I wouldn't have had a clue, but as I had just heard on the radio that a telephone link was shortly to be made between Singapore and the UK, I derived pleasure in displaying my infinite knowledge!

Mr Letty, our 1st Mate on the previous voyage, had been relegated to an old Blue Funneller and paid us a visit. When he first came on board, he was enthusiastic about his new ship and spoke of her beautiful all-wooden decks. But, with a few gins inside him, he expressed regret at losing the *Glengarry* which, he was well aware, was due to his over fondness for the beverage he was imbibing. Although born in Thirkleby, near Thirsk, in Yorkshire, he said he been brought up in Rogart, in Sutherland, and asked for my atlas so that he could show me where it was. And when I handed him the atlas, he underlined the name in ink. As I always take care of books, this annoyed me, but the mark exists to remind me of Letty whom I liked. Although Letty rose to become Master, I was told that he ended up behind the counter of his own grocer's shop in Auchterarder.

I bought a newspaper almost every day in the Malayan ports and the following is a selection of the items they carried:

Malaya Tribune - Penang, Friday, March 17, 1950 - 'Winston Churchill told Parliament yesterday that Western Europe cannot be successfully defended against possible invasion by Russia without active aid of Western Germany.' - Writing in the Manchester Guardian, Sir John Pratt, former British propaganda chief in the Far East, 'charged that the air raids by Nationalist planes were made by "America's friends" and have 'driven the Chinese Reds into Stalin's arms. He added that the United States "recognizes a gang of bandits who have taken refuge on Formosa and who obtain from America arms and money required for their piratical raids upon the Chinese people."' - 'One of Japan's leading Communists told a Red rally here (Tokyo) on Wednesday night that America is plotting a third world war and warned the Japanese people against letting the United States colonise Japan and retain military bases here after a peace treaty is signed'. - A picture on the front page was captioned, 'The funeral in Batu Gajah recently of the four BOR's who were victims of the ambush at Cameron Highlands. The Union Jack draped coffins are seen being borne by Army personnel to the cemetery.'

The Sunday Times - Singapore, Sunday, March 19, 1950 - 'Martial law may be imposed..... The question of appointing a Commander-in-Chief of anti-bandit operations has, it is understood, been referred by the Government (in Kuala Lumpur) to Whitehall and the War Office.....At present, operations against the bandits are decided by the police in the first instance, with the Army in the role of assisting the civil power.' - 'Found without an identity card at Singkang, a notorious bandit area along the

Jementah-Muar road, 35-yer-old Wong Ah Jong today was sentenced to seven months' hard labour.....' - 'About 200 Communist pamphlets, the most found in Penang since the emergency, were found yesterday in the Chung Ling High School.....The pamphlets, printed in Chinese were found strewn on the floor of every classroom'. - 'For the first time in a quarter of a century, planters in Malaya now have a satisfactory price for their rubber.....' - 'The spraying of rural houses in the Federation with DDT and BHC as experiments in malaria control is proving successful.' - An advertisement for Brylcream, captioned 'Set for the day', showed Denis Compton with his hair held beautifully in place while batting!

The Straits Times - Singapore, Monday, March 20, 1950 - 'Reports from Shanghai said Chinese Communist officials, apparently feeling a loss of face over the prospective big foreign exodus aboard the General Gordon, have been delaying issuing exit visas.' - 'The Vietminh Command in Southern Indo-China has ordered its troops to fire on any American aircraft flying over the territory.'

The Straits Times - Singapore, Wednesday, March 22, 1950 - 'The Federation Government announced today that it has appointed Lieut-Gen. Sir Harold Rawdon Briggs, KCIE, CB, CBE, DSO, Indian Army (retired), as Director of Operations, to plan, co-ordinate and generally direct the anti-bandit operations of the police and fighting forces. The post is a civil one.' - 'Three Europeans - two miners and a British police sergeant - and an Indian police driver were killed and two police constables, three specials, and a Malay driver were wounded, in two ambushes in different parts of Kedah this morning.'

The Straits Times - Singapore, Thursday, March 23, 1950 - 'Police disguised as bandits started off an operation last night which ended this morning in an engagement between nearly 200 police and men of the 1st Suffolk Regiment and, it is believed, two armed bandits in a squatter area four miles outside Kuala Lumpur. One Chinese bandit armed with a pistol, a Chinese woman member of the Malayan Communist Party and a 10-year-old boy were killed. The security forces suffered five casualties - a British cadet police officer, a sergeant and two privates of the Suffolks and a Malay police constable. They were all wounded.' - A photograph on the front page was captioned 'Men of the 1st Suffolks carrying out the body of a bandit killed in a battle between troops and bandits yesterday at the 4th mile Cheras Road, just outside Kuala Lumpur.' (Two soldiers carried the pole from which the dead man hung by his arms and legs and the leading soldier smiled for the camera.) - 'A European Anti-Bandit

Month squad leader, Mr E.W. Mathis, was among nine casualties injured last night in Penang's second handgrenade explosion within a week.' - 'The War Minster, Mr John Strachey, told Parliament yesterday that urgent steps had been taken to comply with the demand of the military authorities in Malaya for additional supplies of armoured vehicles.' - 'A Chinese carrying a basket of fresh cooked rice was stopped by a jungle squad sergeant in the Sungei Patani area of Kedah yesterday. After struggling free and ignoring a challenge to halt, the man was shot and killed.' 'The Government yesterday emphatically rejected flogging as the answer to Britain's present crime wave.' - An advertisement for Philips Lamps showed a picture of the "Willem Ruys" and was captioned 'M.V. Willem Ruys fully equipped from stem to stern with Philips Lighting.....'

The following letter appeared in Saturday's Straits Times: 'Your lead story of Thursday morning, under the heading "200 Men in Battle Outside K.L.," must have induced some very strong feelings among readers. When I read the first paragraph in it, I concluded that a printing error had occurred, and that, instead of "two armed bandits," "two armed bands" had been intended. Having finished the story, I regret to say, I was astounded to discover that there was no error. In fact, nearly 200 police and men of the 1st Suffolk regiment, armed with rifles, two flame throwers, Brens and carbines, two-inch mortars and hand grenades, were held in an "engagement" with, as far as I can discover, two men, a woman and a child armed with a shot gun, a pistol, some food, cooking utensils, Communist pamphlets, eggs, school books, a pencil, eraser and a ruler. The bandits suffered three killed, our forces received five casualties. I do not underestimate the difficulties of jungle fighting - a small force is unbelievably elusive - but I do not consider your article one generally calculated to spread confidence. In fact, I think that if I had the misfortune to be a bandit, a copy would possess a place of honour in my scrap book. (Signed) John St. John. Singapore.

The Straits Times - Singapore, Friday, March 24, 1950 - 'Famine Spreads To Half China. Parents Sell Their Children To Buy Food.' - 'Vietnamese police and French troops were today ordered to remain in a "state of alert" as a fresh wave of terrorism swept over the town (Saigon).' - 'Australia today invoked far-reaching emergency powers - including the right of immediate arrest, the banning of meetings and the death penalty for treason - to fight labour disorders and Communism.' - 'Belgium, without government and with bigger strikes threatened, faced a new crisis last night over the issue of King Leopold's return.' - 'Chinese Nationalists warplanes hit Shanghai again, concentrating on Lunghwa airport, the runway of which is said to be unusable from repeated raids.' - 'Britain is doing her best to restore stable government in Burma, the Foreign Secretary, Mr Ernest Bevin, told Parliament yesterday.' - 'Seretse Khama, claimant to the Bamangwato chieftainship, last night accused the British Government of wanting to get rid of him so that it could resort to direct rule of his territory (Bechuanaland).' (Renamed Botswana in 1966 when it became independent with Sir Seretse as its first president). - 'A former British army chief in Tokyo said yesterday that Japan's "potential threat to the British textile industry is a very big one."'

The Straits Times - Singapore, Saturday, March 25, 1950 - 'While famine stalks through half of China, including the most densely populated areas, train-loads of cereals have been seen passing Nanking for the north-eastern provinces, presumably in exchange for railroad equipment and other machinery from Russia.' - 'Portuguese troops clashed with the Chinese Communists earlier this week, killed four Reds and brought Peking fury down on the tiny colony of Macao. A Macao report said five launches of Red soldiers tried to reach a group of Nationalists who had taken refuge in Macao.' - 'The 300,000-strong Indonesian Seamen's Union is backing a new national shipping company named Jakarta Lloyd which has been set up in Jakarta to compete with the Dutch shipping line KPM.' - 'After an absence of more than three years, King Phumiphon Aduldet of Siam arrived back in his country today and was given a most enthusiastic welcome by his subjects.' - 'A thousand workers, whose strikes have paralysed Brisbane, today decided to continue their strikes, despite the risk of prison sentences under the Crimes Act. The Australian Government, which invoked the Crimes act yesterday, has decided, according to a report from Canberra, to prosecute immediately the men's leaders who continue to advocate strike action.' - 'Women are not allowed to mix with men in the mosques for moral reasons, said Inche Ahmad Ibrahim, vice-president of the Singapore Muslim Advisory Board. "Our attention may be distracted," he added. "Instead of praying men might be watching the women."'

15   HONG KONG

We left Singapore at 11.12am on Saturday 25 March. It was Grand National Day at Aintree and Mrs Savery, her daughter, Elsa and two or three other passengers asked if they could come to the wireless room to listen to the broadcast as they found it difficult to tune in the BBC on the set in the lounge. The broadcast came through loud and clear; it was apparently a beautiful day in Liverpool and Freebooter, ridden by J Power, won by fifteen lengths from Wot No Sun, ridden by AP Thompson.

Dick and I stood listening with the others although we had no interest in the race. When it ended, the passengers thanked us and departed. That is, all except Elsa who perhaps also had no interest in the race, but took advantage of the opportunity to have a talk with young men close to her own age. It was one of those beautiful nights at sea, with the stars twinkling in the firmament, and we were enjoying the chat when Mrs Savery reappeared at the door and told Elsa that it was 'time she was coming'. And, when Elsa hesitated, Mrs Savery glared at her and she dutifully followed her mother. I didn't have much to do with the Saverys, but they were in the Captain's cabin one day when he told me to do something and I made a note of it in shorthand. Elsa, who was engaged to an Army Captain in Hong Kong, later asked what qualifications, in addition to shorthand, I had to have to be purser. I doubt if there was another in Holt's fleet who knew shorthand and the answer was a PMG Certificate in Wireless Telegraphy!

Regarding radio reception, the time signals sent on 16 kcs long-wave by the powerful transmitter in Rugby could still be heard faintly in Japan.

We docked at Holt's Wharf in Kowloon at 1.39pm on Wednesday, 29 March and R. Silsby, Supernumerary Carpenter, signed off for transferral to the *Patroclus*.

Dick and I decided to spend the evening ashore. It was dark as we alighted from the gangway and Mr Horan, who was working on the quay, approached us. "What this?" he asked, "You can't go ashore together when we're working cargo." I thought at first that he was joking, but Horan, who wasn't much for joking, was deadly serious and quoted Holt's Rule Book. I had never heard of such a thing and, anyway would not have been irresponsible if something had required to be done. We returned up the gangway, up the stairs to the passengers' deck, then up to the boat deck and straight to Captain MacTavish's cabin. He ushered us in and, in support of our complaint, I pointed out that Mr Horan had quoted the Rule Book which stated that the 1st Mate was responsible for surveying damaged cargo, but had never done so and left it to Dick. This, of course, was normal practice, but once you start quoting a rulebook.....! MacTavish, a kindly man, tried to placate us and said he would speak to Mr Horan.

We were sitting in my cabin when Horan came in and sat talking to us. It was then that I learned that he had been on the *Anchises* when she was attacked in on her the way to Shanghai and that Amos W. Parkin, my No.1 on the *Samforth*, had also been on board. The 'going ashore together' incident was not referred to and Horan made no comment when we went together in Japan.

We sailed, for Taku Bar, near Tientsin in the Gulf of Chihli (Po Hai), at 4.48pm on Friday, 31 March. And the following evening, a precedent having been set, a gentleman passenger asked if he could listen to the Oxford and Cambridge Boat Race in the wireless room. Again we tuned in the BBC Overseas Service and, when Cambridge won and the man disclosed that he had been to the University, we promptly christened him 'The Grad'.

16   TAKU BAR

As the Chinese Revolution was still in progress and we were bound for a Communist-held port, we were instructed to maintain radio silence - apart from sending our daily noon position on short-wave, using the anti-piracy code, to Commodore Hong Kong. We, therefore, slipped out of Hong Kong without indicating our departure to Hong Kong Radio (VPS) and, again displaying the Union Jack on No.3 hatch, made as if heading for Japan via the Bashi Channel. As before, this route took us east of Formosa (Taiwan) and when Dick heard the *Breconshire*, returning from Japan, on the air, he did not make our presence known.

We were in the Yellow Sea (Hwang-Hai) when I went looking for Captain MacTavish to get him to sign a document. I located him on the bridge looking through binoculars and when I told him what I wanted, he said "Not at the moment, please, Mr Malcolm" and I then saw that he was focussed on a large battleship which I could just make out through the prevailing mist. The ship was never identified, but was believed to be a Soviet warship.

We anchored at Taku Bar at 7.18pm on Tuesday, 4 April, 1950 and Dick closed down the station without informing Tientsin Radio (XSV) as he would normally have done. Remaining in the wireless room, however, he switched the receiver on again and, hearing XSV calling us (GNCS) on 500 kcs, started up the transmitter, answered, and copied the message. But, when he delivered it to Captain MacTavish, the Agent was present and complained that we should have received it several days previously, Duncan put him in his place with all due pomposity!

Tientsin (Tianjin or T'ien-ching), the port for Peking (Beijing), stands on the Grand Canal, thirty-two miles from the Gulf of Chihli. Ships such as the *Glengarry*, however, were too large for the Canal and were handled at Taku Bar. Even then, the shore was in the distance and cargo was brought out in lighters. I photographed the first one to arrive. It was fairly large with a mast amidships and a small funnel at the stern. The latter, however, is likely to have been a galley funnel, as it was pulled by a tug smaller than itself.

When the tug came alongside, I was surprised to see seven European men standing on its deck. All were well dressed; six in clothes of a casual nature, such as bomber jackets with fur collars, while one, whose fur-lined coat hung open, wore a lounge suit and collar and tie. They proved to be tally clerks and White Russians; or rather the children of White Russians. And, that being the case, I wondered what they thought of finding themselves living in a country which now embraced the very doctrine from which their parents had fled in 1917. The men I spoke to were well educated and could speak English. I was told that life for the majority had improved under the Communists as now, with wages being partly paid in food, everyone was at least being fed.

The Government were obviously trying to give jobs to as many people as possible and an absolute swarm of workers boarded the ship, plus an armed soldier with the Red Star of China on his cap. I was at my desk when a man carrying a clip-board, stepped into my cabin and, using sign-language, asked if it would be all right if he sat down on the settee to write. Thinking that he merely wanted to make a brief note, I smiled and gave him permission. But, as the time passed and he remained seated, it dawned on me that he considered himself permanently settled and I kicked him out. He was anything but pleased and, when I later heard of Europeans being taken ashore and imprisoned, I realized that my action could have led to trouble.

Most of the so-called workers had nothing to do. They installed themselves in the officers' smoke room next door to my cabin and, during their occupation, the name of the room was never more appropriate as they smoked incessantly so that it contained a dense fug. They remained there, playing cards, both day and night, and I could hear the racket when I was trying to sleep. Bureaucracy was rife in China; normally I had to supply two crew lists, or three at the most. In Taku Bar, they required something like eight!

The cargo which we loaded consisted of bales and cases of silk, bags of apricot kernels, cases of bristles, bales of goat hair, pheasants, china grass, duck feathers, drums of stillingia oil, wood oil, peppermint oil, casks of hog casings and cases of tea.

Europeans were desperate to get out of China and would travel long distances to board any ship which would get them out. Missionaries were, of course, superfluous to the new regime and eight German nuns, an Anglican bishop and an American banker boarded before we sailed at 10.42am on Thursday, 6 April. As Mrs Savery and her daughter were still with us, this made up our full complement of passengers.

I do not recall how the radio station at Mokpo, in [13]Korea, knew of our presence, but, we were in the Yellow Sea and I was with Dick in the wireless room, when Mokpo Radio (HLM) called us and asked for our position. We informed the bridge and Captain MacTavish joined us in the wireless room. When he expressed doubt about divulging our position by saying that he wouldn't have minded if they had asked later in the evening, I said, "How about giving our evening position, sir?" "That's what I was thinking, Mr Malcolm," he replied and this is what was done.

---

[13] Japan annexed Korea in 1910 and the country remained part of the Japanese Empire until Japan surrendered to the Allies in 1945. The country was then divided into a Soviet Occupied Zone, north of the 38th parallel, and a southern zone, occupied by US Forces. In 1948, the Soviet Zone became the (communist) Democratic People's Republic and the American Zone became the (capitalist) Republic of (South) Korea. On 25 June, 1950, the Korean War began, when the North invaded the South, and continued until an Armistice was signed between UN and North Korean Commanders (and Chinese People's 'volunteers') in 1953. However, as South Korea did not sign the Armistice Agreement and a Peace Treaty has still not been signed, the war is, technically, still in progress and US forces continue to patrol the border between the two countries.

17   JAPAN

The American banker came to the wireless room with a telegram to his friend Admiral Turner Joy, in Japan, and Dick sent it on H/F (high frequency/short wave) to JCS, the Japanese equivalent of Portishead in the UK. And, as the telegram was paid for in US dollars and as this was a new currency for us, Duncan had to provide a new tin! While talking to the Bishop, who, I seem to remember, had been Bishop of Tientsin, Dick mentioned that he had attended the China Inland Mission School in Chefoo in the 1920s when Miss Kendon had been head mistress. The Bishop knew Miss Kendon and said that, now in her eighties, she was living in Australia.

We docked in Yokohama at 2.54pm on Sunday, 9 April and left at 6.18pm the following day. Nagoya was reached at 8.12am on the 11th and I was sitting at the piano in the afternoon when a young man appeared at the door of the smoke room. He had a limited knowledge of English, we chatted and he gave me his card on which was printed Y. O'GINO, Aichi Kaiun K.K., Sub-Agent for Isbrandtsen Line, New York. As he was a friendly chap, I gave him a tin of fifty cigarettes and, much to my surprise, he returned the next morning with a bunch of flowers and a couple of old music books. From our western view, the flowers were, of course, an embarrassment. And, having nowhere to put them, I crammed them through the narrow neck of my water bottle and all the boys had a good laugh. I corresponded my Japanese friend for several years and, on a Christmas Card he wrote - 'Dear Jan-san, I was very sorry for you during in 1951 for the idleness of my pen. But it was sure that I didn't forget you, so I write down here a apology from the bottom of my heart.' It is easy to laugh at a foreigner's English, which is often very funny, while tending to forget that they are the ones who attempt to master a foreign language. Dick and I used to greet each other with "Hullo for you, I am seeing you before" which was how a dockworker greeted me in Singapore. And, once, when we were leaving Aden, the Agent's clerk said, "Mr Purser, everything is now completely"!

Held together by glue, only one of the pair of Satsuma vases, which I bought during a visit to Nagoya, is in my house now. In retirement, my father always did the dusting in the house and, much to his dismay, he broke one of the vases, but glued the pieces back together. He predeceased my mother by five years and after she died in 1989 and the undamaged vase was found to be missing, it was suspected that the home help had broken it and quietly disposed of the pieces.

We sailed at 12.51pm on the 12th and arrived in Kobe at 8am on the 13th. During a trip ashore in the afternoon, I managed to get a recording of 'China Night'; the tune played by the musical box I had bought in Otaru the previous voyage. On the rim of the label of the 78 rpm record, it states, in English, 'Made By Nippon Columbia Co. Ltd. Kawasaki, Japan. But, as all the other information is in Japanese, I now wonder how the shop assistant knew what I wanted.

When I was working at my desk one evening, I clerk brought documents for me to sign. I don't recollect what they were, but they concerned the cargo and, after I signed the first one, he gave me the carbon copy. I did not want it and told him so, but, when he insisted, I tore it up and dropped it into my wastepaper basket. Such behaviour shocked the man who displayed his astonishment by a sharp intake of breath through closed teeth as each of the others was dealt with in similar fashion!

Cargo was discharged and loaded at each of these ports. In Yokohama, we loaded cases and bales of pongee silk; in Nagoya, porcelain, oak planks and plywood and, in Kobe, cotton piece goods, bamboo poles and general cargo. We sailed at 7.54pm on Saturday, 15 April.

18   HONG KONG HOMEWARD

We anchored in Hong Kong harbour at 9am on the 19th and the front page headline of The Hong Kong Telegraph of Thursday, 20 April, 1950 read: 'Lightning Dock Strike Threatening To Paralyse London Port'. The article, dated April 19, went on to say 'By tonight nearly 2,000 dockers and stevedores loading and discharging 16 vessels in the biggest docks (the Royal Group) of the port had stopped work.' There were two reasons for the dispute. The main one being that the Transport and General Workers' Union had expelled three men who had led the unofficial strike the previous summer and the other one was that a shipping company intended to change the conditions of work of stevedores. The strike escalated, servicemen (5000) were again moved in and, by 26 April, 14,441 workers (more than half the labour force) were out so that only 23 ships were being handled and 81 lay idle. On Thursday, 27 April, the Dock Labour Board issued the ultimatum that, unless the strikers returned by Monday morning, their services would be terminated. This had the desired effect. The unofficial strike began to crumble and, when the leaders saw this, they called it off.

Regarding trade union activities in Hong Kong, the Telegraph reported that three men, who had wounded a non-union man for refusing to join, were each sentenced to 'nine years' hard labour and 18 strokes'.

Other items in the newspaper were: The Chinese Nationalist Navy operating from Taiwan had captured the *Ethel Moller* and *Tai Ping Yan* and the British Consul there was 'pressing for the release of the crews if not of the ships'. - The Corinth Canal, which had only recently opened after being blocked by the retreating German Army, had been blocked by an earthquake. - Victims of the cholera epidemic in Calcutta were so numerous that they were 'dying faster than they could be counted'.

The *Glengyle* lay close to us and I went across to visit Ron Gallop who had been my No. 1 on my first voyage on the *Glengarry*. We had lunch together on board and were chatting on deck afterwards when the 3rd Mate passed and Ron mentioned that he also came from Dundee and that his name was Ray. But, as they didn't acknowledge each other, I didn't make myself known. J.C. Ray, whose initials must have occasionally been remarked upon, hit the headlines in 1970 when, as Master of the *Anchises*, he was arrested and held for over three weeks for allegedly violating harbour regulations on the way into Shanghai.

When he went ashore, Desmond Stewart wore silk shirts which I admired, as his initials DHS were embroidered on the left breast. As he had bought them in Hong Kong, I asked a trader who came on board to provide a similar shirt for me. Language was a difficulty, but I drew my initials IMM, in italic form, on a piece of paper and explained, more than once, that I didn't want the letters copied exactly as I had written them; I wanted a good job. When he returned with the shirt, the letters were exactly as I had written them. I refused the shirt and later regretted doing so. I wouldn't have had any pleasure in wearing it, but I should have considered the lady who had gone to so much trouble.

I had previously bought a silk dressing gown for myself from Old Swatow and went again to his shop to get one for my father. When I was about to leave after buying the article, it was raining cats and dogs and Swatow said I should take a rickshaw back to the ship (as rickshaws had covers). But I had spent every cent I had and, when I told him this, he offered me a dollar saying that I could pay him back next time I was in Hong Kong. As I didn't think I would be back, I told him so, but he forced the dollar on me.

The cargo loaded, from lighters, consisted of cotton piece goods, goose feathers, duck feathers, sea grass, graphite, aniseed, sewing needles, cassia, cassia oil, peppermint oil, citronella oil, stillingia oil, teaseed oil, mustard seed oil, hog casings, bamboo, egg yolk, green tea, mats, canes, skins, stem ginger, naval stores, mail, handkerchiefs, personal effects and 195 cases of bullion.

As Hong Kong is an entrepôt, most of the above was brought from China by smaller ships for transhipment to Europe. Notable among the latter were those of the China Navigation Co., Ltd. whose ships, such as the *Wusueh* on their River Service, used the long navigable rivers to go into the very heart of the country. I mentioned that we used the anti-piracy code to send our position to Commodore, Hong Kong when on passage to Taku Bar and, by 1950, most people believed that piracy had long been relegated to history. This was far from the case on the China coast and the coastal ships were recognisable by large metal spikes protruding from their central accommodation. A favourite ploy of the pirates was to board as deck passengers, with a view to taking over the ship at sea, and the spikes were to make this more difficult.

The following item appeared in the Trade And Transport Section of the South China Morning Post of Sunday, July 17, 1949 under the heading

'Piracy Story'. 'How the *Kwei Hwa*, of 350 net tons and carrying about 350 passengers, was pirated on Wednesday night was described by Mr Fan Mui, the chief officer of the ship which arrived in Hongkong yesterday. The vessel left Canton at 9.27 p.m. for Hongkong. At 10.55 p.m. six pirates, armed with revolvers, machine-guns and hand-grenades, broke into the wheelhouse from the bow. Six more pirates were at the rear of the ship, which was completely controlled by them within a few minutes. The master, Capt Ho Ping-cheung, the first and second officers, the pilot and quarter-master, were covered and they were ordered to steer the vessel astern. The ship reached Tai Shan at 11.05 p.m. and it was run aground at the orders of the pirates, who then started to unload the cargo which comprised oil, tea and general cargo and was valued at about $10,000. The personal effects of the passengers and crew, valued at about $100,000, were also taken. The pirates left at 1.40 a.m., taking with them the captain, the purser, Leung King-chor, and about ten passengers as hostages. The ship had to wait till 3.30 a.m. when the tide rose enough to enable her to refloat. She then returned to Canton.....She is registered in China.....The pirates posed as passengers on board.' Piracy still exists and is perhaps even worse today, particularly in West Africa and Indonesia.

PHOTOGRAPHS

With the nurses at the Serpentine, Hyde Park, London.

Dick Molland, Chu Ching Fah and me.

White Russians about to board, Taku Bar.

Working cargo in Japan.

Road repairing, Nagoya.

Girl workers, Nagoya.

In the Smoke Room.

Glengarry in Singapore.

In Singapore.

With Dick on the bridge, Boxing Day, 1949.

Mount Lavinia.

With Chen Ying Yueh (left) and Chu Ching Foo.

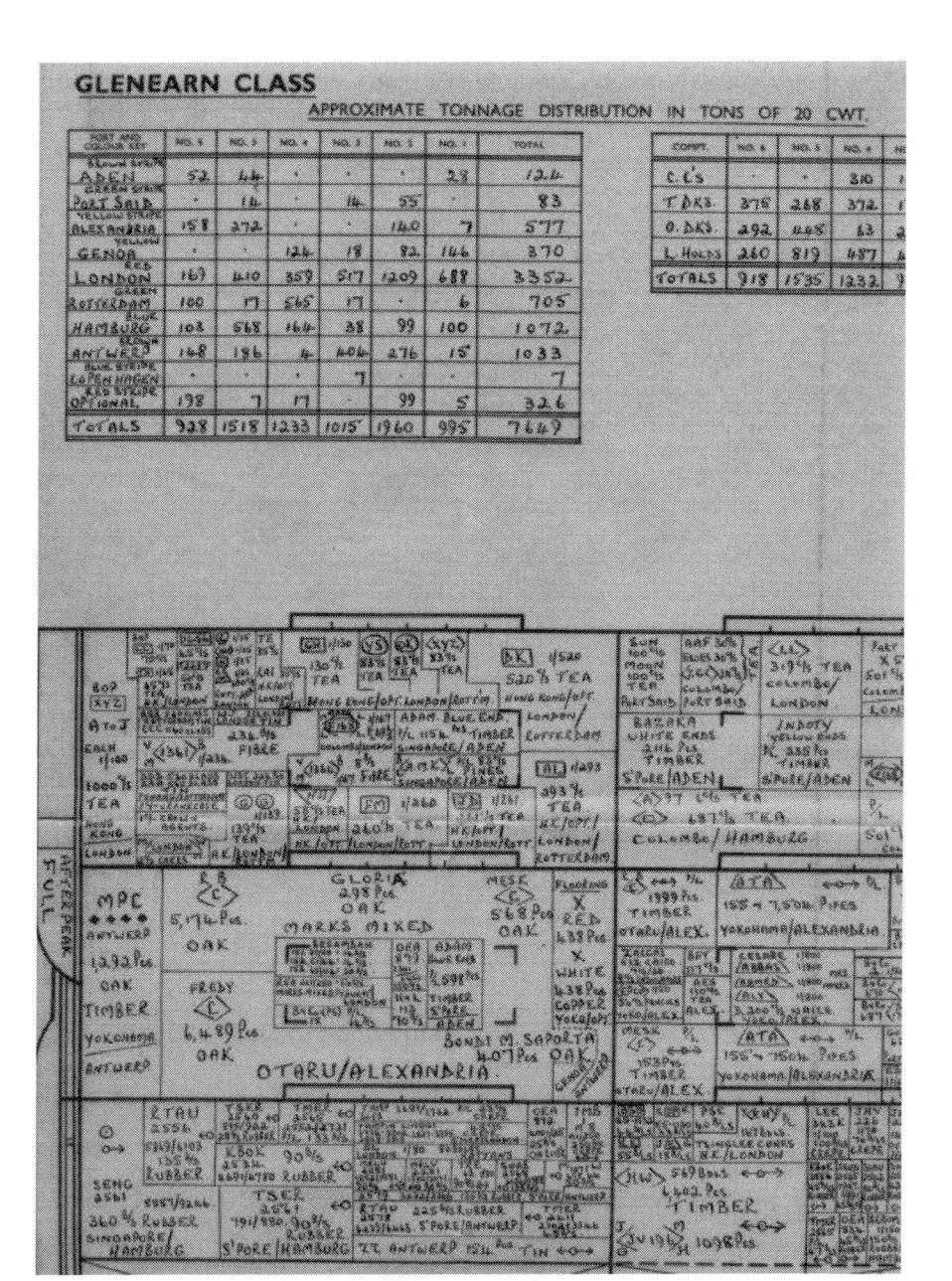

Section of home cargo plan, Voyage 7.

Standing between my cabin (left) and the Wireless Room.

Section of my cabin.

Leaving King George V Dock, London, bound Rotterdam.

With Clare at Airborne Cemetery, Oosterbeek, near Arnhem.

Section of Airborne Cemetery.

British and Chinese crew leaving the Glenfinlas, KGV London.

Patroclus, Bellerophon, King David and Titan, King George V Dock, Shieldhall, Glasgow.

With Marie Crabb, Kelvingrove, Glasgow.

Canal tours, Amsterdam.

Amsterdam

Volendam.

With Volendam ladies.

Crossing to Marken.

Children, Marken.

Watching the fishing fleet departing, Marken.

Clare in Delft.

Section of Panorama Mesdag, The Hague.

With Clare, Houses of Parliament, The Hague.

On the promenade, Scheveningen.

With Helen, The Embankment, London

19   MALAYA

We sailed at 1pm on Tuesday, 25 April and anchored in the Eastern Roads at Singapore at 8.30pm on Friday, the 28th. Mrs Savery and Elsa, who were transferring to another ship to continue their holiday, in Australia, signed off the following day. It was 5.30pm on Sunday the 30th before we berthed beside the *Antilochus* and loading began. As always, the main cargo consisted of numerous consignments of rubber destined for various European ports, but we also loaded thousands of pieces of timber, thousands of cases of pineapples, yang planks, rubber footwear, drums of latex and coconut oil, bales of hemp, bags of palm kernels, tapioca, sago flour, white and black pepper and ore, cases of bush shirts and fish maws, stationery, a car belonging to C.W. Dawson and personal effects.

It may have been on this occasion that a docker was injured when he was crushed between a swinging bale of rubber and a godown. And, as regards safety, you always had to be careful when a ship was working cargo; not only because slings were swinging in the air, but also because wires and ropes were strewn across the main decks. An unwritten law was that you should never jump onto a covered hatch on the assumption that the hatch boards were in place beneath the cover. If they weren't, you could drop into the hold. Another unwritten law applied when a ship was at sea and which is expressed by the adage 'Only fools and midshipmen (meaning novices who knew no better) sit on rails'. Ron Gallop told me about an incident which had occurred on the *Glengarry* before I joined her. The ship was in the Mediterranean when a midshipman, who had been sitting on the rail chatting with one or two others, lost his balance and fell into the sea. Fortunately, the sea the calm, the ship was stopped and the lad brought back on board. Everyone watched as the embarrassed youth climbed the gangway, but, much to his surprise, he was not immediately given a dressing down. Captain Anderson was wise enough to know that the lad would be suffering from shock. But he did send for him the next day!

Another accident of a less serious nature occurred one evening in Singapore. Keen to hear the record of 'China Night' I had bought in Kobe, I was just stepping over the coaming of my cabin, on my way to the radiogram in the passengers' lounge, when a Chinese seaman appeared, asking for a pass to take something ashore. The record in my hand was in its paper sleeve with the opening, unfortunately, at the bottom. As I turned back into the cabin, the record slipped from the sleeve and was cracked when it fell.

Dick and I were standing in the wireless room one evening when a loud bang caused us both to duck. We might not have known what had caused it if Mr Collyer, the Supernumerary 4th Mate, had not then stepped in to inform us that lightning had struck the main aerial and he had seen a sheet of flame run along its length.

The following is a selection of items in the newspapers:

The Straits Times - Singapore, Monday, May 1, 1950 - 'The Singapore Police have intensified screening operations during the past 48 hours and more than 40,000 people have been checked at road blocks as against the normal 10,000 a day.....Increased police activity follows the bomb attack on the Governor, Sir Franklin Gimson, at the Happy World on Friday night.....' - A picture on the front page carried the caption: 'The Governor of Singapore, Sir Franklin Gimson throws out the first ball at yesterday's baseball game on the padang. A team from the U.S. aircraft carrier Boxer met a combined team from the U.S. destroyers Craig and Parks. It was Sir Franklin's first public appearance since the attempt made on his life.....' - 'Thousands of Chinese were flocking across the Hong Kong border today (Sunday), last day of unrestricted entry to the British Colony. From tomorrow, for the first time since the British took over Hong Kong in 1841, the authorities will treat Chinese from the mainland in the same way as other foreigners and demand travel documents or valid permits of those seeking asylum.....Nearly 30,000 Chinese were believed to have entered the colony in the past week.' - 'More than 700 foreigners have boarded the American liner, General Gordon, off Tientsin in a mass evacuation from Communist China.....' - 'The British freighter Edith Moller returned here (Hong Kong) yesterday from Yulin, where her officers said conditions were "completely chaotic." Unconfirmed reports in the reliable English-language South China Sunday Post said the ship arrived at Hoihow the day before the city fell to the communists. It was forced by the Nationalists to take part in the evacuation to Yulin (on Hainan Island), where it was detained several days. The paper said the arrival at Yulin of the destroyer H.M.S. Constant "changed the attitude of the Nationalist officials" and the Edith Moller was allowed to leave for Hong Kong on Thursday.' - 'A boom in the export of Chinese cotton piecegoods to the South Seas via Hong Kong is expected this year.....Shanghai mills are said to be receiving many inquiries from the Philippines, Malaya, Indonesia, and Siam.....' - 'Italy last night rejected Marshal Tito's (President of Yugoslavia) proposal to exchange the Italian city of Gorizia for Trieste. - 'Official palace sources confirmed yesterday that King Farouk of Egypt wants to marry again. The monarch is anxious to preserve Mohammed Aly's dynasty.....' - 'Seventeen Scots, with a petition having more than 1,000,000 signatures, will go to London soon to demand a separate government for Scotland.' - 'London Dock Strike Ends After 11 days' -

The 'Commercial And Shipping News' section carried the following adverts:

MANSFIELD & CO., LTD.
(Incorporated in Singapore)

BLUE FUNNEL LINE
Carrier's option to proceed via other ports to load and discharge cargo.

SAILINGS to LIVERPOOL, GLASGOW, LONDON & CONTINENTAL PORTS.

Rhesus for L'pool, Avonmouth& Holland…..
Due   Sails   P. S'ham   Penang
G.25/26   May 8   May 9/10   May 11/12
Antilochus for Genoa, Marseilles, Liverpool & Glasgow......
G.34/35   May 3   May 4/5   May 6/7
Glaucus for P. Sudan/Tunis Holland/London....
May 7   May 10   May 13/15   May 15
Autolycus for Casablanca, Liverpool & Glasgow…..
May 11   May 17
Mentor for L'pool & Havre
May 16   May 20   May 21/22   May 23/24
Perseus for Liverpool...
May 17   May 26   May 27/28   May 29/30

SAILINGS to and from BRISBANE, SYDNEY, MELBOURNE, ADELAIDE.

Idomeneus… May 24   June 10   May30/June 1   June 2/3

SAILINGS to and from W. AUSTRALIA.
Gorgon due from Fremantle..   G.11
Sails for Fremantle........   May 6
SAILINGS from U.K., U.S.A.
Astyanax due from U.K......   May 2
Pyrrhus due from U.K.......   May 7

Elpenor due from U.K..........	May 8	
Herefordshire due from U.S.A...	May 8	(This was, in fact, a Bibby Line ship)
Talthybius due from U.K........	May 13	
Polydorus due from U.S.A......	May 21	
Rhexenor due from U.K........	May 23	

BLUE FUNNEL
Monthly North American Service
- to -
Halifax (Montreal), Boston, New York, Baltimore, Philadelphia, New Orleans and Galveston.

	S'pore	P.S'ham	Penang
Melampus....	-	-	29 Apr./2 May

Agents:-

ANGLO-FRENCH & BENDIXSENS LTD.

BOUSTEAD & CO., LTD.
Lloyd Agents:
Ticket Agents for Malayan Railway.

GLEN LINE
From U.K. & Continental Ports for Hong Kong & Japan

Glenroy	Due	Sails
Penang..........	In Port	1 May
P. S'ham........	2 May	3 May
S'pore...........	4 May	8 May
*Denbighshire due Penang		13 May

A fortnightly service for Colombo, Aden, London, Rotterdam, Antwerp & Hamburg.

Glengarry *	Due	Sails
S'pore....	Eastern Roads	4 May
P.S'ham........	5 May	6 May
Penang........	7 May	7 May
Radnorshire+.....	11 May	16 May
Glengyle.....	25 May	1 June

* Calls Tangier, Casablanca + Genoa

Carriers Option to proceed to other Ports to load and discharge cargo.

BEN LINE STEAMERS LTD.
For U.K./Continent:

Benlawers for L'pool, G'gow, Dublin, Havre, Antwerp, Rotterdam…
| S'pore | P. S'ham | Penang |
| G. 6/7 | In Port | 2-3 May |

Benvannoch for Avonmouth, London, Hamburg, Leith, Hull...
In Port   10 May   11 May

Benattow for London, Antwerp, Rotterdam, M'brough...
7-13 May   14-15 May   16-18 May

Bennevis for Genoa, L'pool, A'mouth, Havre, Rotterdam, Hamburg...
25-29 May   30 May   31 May-2 June

Bencruachan for L'pool, Glasgow, Dublin, Antwerp, Rotterdam...
24-29 May   30-31 May   1-3 June

Bencleuch for London, Antwerp, Rotterdam, Hamburg, Hull...
G. 38/39   4-5 June   6-8 June

From U.K..Continent Bencleuch for H'Kong, Manila, Cebu, Sandakan...
In Port

Benwyvis for H'Kong, Japan, Sandakan, Tawao...
4-9 May   In Port

To and from Bangkok:
Benveg due from Bangkok.... ….   10 May

G = Godown/warehouse.
The Ben Line, owned by Wm. Thomson & Co. of Leith, was Holt's competitor in the Far East.

The Malay Tribune - Singapore, Wednesday, May 3, 1950 - 'Rubber Word War Starts. US Demands Cheaper Price At Brussels.....An American delegate said that among the first points the U.S. delegation will bring forward was the "sky high price" of crude rubber, now up to 26 (US) cents per pound.....' - 'Tappers Ignore May Day. Estate labourers in Negri Sembilan refused to take heed of Red posters and verbal threats and turned out in full force for work, yesterday.' - 'Powerful rocket installations aimed at Alaska, Norway and Sweden have been built in Russia in the Arctic and Baltic areas, says a 33-year-old escapee from a Soviet concentration camp.' - 'The British (Labour) Government announced today that it did not intend to introduce a bill to outlaw the Communist Party.' - 'General Douglas MacArthur believes that many Japanese prisoners of war remain in Russian hands despite the Russian announcement that repatriation had been completed.....' - 'Justice Minister C. R. Swart said today that a "strong and wide" bill designed to dissolve South Africa's small Communist movement will probably be tabled in Parliament on Friday.' - 'The Communist-led "Freedom Movement" which organised a May Day strike and demonstrations in Transvaal, today blamed the Government for last night's riots in which 18 Africans were killed.' - 'Malan Wants To Quit The C'wealth.....Prime Minister Daniel Malan told the Senate today that India's decision to become a Republic "means that if we wanted to become a Republic then we could become that without isolation and without revolution".'- 'The Shu-Tung-Wen Romanisation of the Chinese characters will not only bring the Chinese language within easier reach of foreigners but also solve the problem of illiteracy among the masses in China.' - 'The Shanghai Dockyards, one of the leading British enterprises in Shanghai, reported a loss of HK$1,317,000 for the year ended September 30th last.' - 'Nationalist China today officially announced that Hainan Island, their last major air and sea blockade base outside Formosa itself, was completely in Chinese Communist hands.' - 'A special investigation committee of the United National (Government) Party has recommended the Ceylon Government to purge Communists from civil service, Government schools and rural development societies.' - 'The 20,000-ton Cunard liner Scythia, fully reconditioned, will return to North Atlantic service in August.....' - 'With the holiday period about to begin thousands of Britons are preparing to spend their annual fortnight abroad.....many of them will be "freshmen" taking their holiday outside England for the first time.....nearly all will be going either to the continent or to the Channel Islands.....All, too, will be faced with the same problem of keeping their expenditure within the upper limit of £50, which is the maximum amount of sterling allowed to British tourists.'

We sailed from Singapore at 11.30am on Saturday, 6 May and docked in Port Swettenham at 8am the next day. Having loaded more rubber and 4467 pieces of timber, we left at 7.30pm the same day. Penang was reached about noon on Monday, 8 May, but we didn't go alongside. When we lay at anchor, an invitation was received from [14]HMS *London* for the master and officers of the *Glengarry* to come over for drinks in the evening. I would love to have gone, but we sailed, for Colombo, at 6.15pm.

---

[14] The 1929-built cruiser was broken up in Barrow-in-Furness later in the year.

20   THE LAST LEG

We anchored in Colombo harbour at 8.9pm on Thursday, 11 May and the following afternoon a Singhalese Immigration official came to my cabin asking for Sir Patrick McKerron who, with his wife, had boarded in Penang. Thinking nothing of it, I asked Dick to tell Sir Patrick that he was wanted, but this threw the official into a panic. "No," he said, "*I* will go to see *him*." Having loaded cases of tea, bales of rubber, drums of latex, bags of plumbago, cases of desiccated coconut and bales of coir yarn, we sailed at 8.12am on Saturday.

The work of preparing the cargo plans and cargo books, for posting in Aden, was begun as soon as we left Penang and, on this occasion, the plan contained the following information:

GLEN LINE LTD.
m.v. "GLENGARRY" VOY. 8 HOMEWARD
Sailed from (First Loading Port) TAKU BAR on 6th April, 1950
Sailed from (Second Loading Port)   YOKOHAMA on 10th April, 1950
Sailed from (Last Loading Port)   COLOMBO on 13th May, 1950
Draft Leaving Last Loading Port:- Forwd. 28'0" Aft. 30'7"
Fuel Oil Last Loading Port:- 716.5 tons

For:- Yokohama: Nagoya: Kobe: Hong Kong: Singapore: Port Swettenham: Penang: Colombo: Aden: Port Said: Tangier: Casablanca: London: Rotterdam: Hamburg: Antwerp.
The tonnage for the ports was as follows:
Aden - 206. Port Said - 50. Tangier - 40. Casablanca - 19. London - 5280.
Rotterdam - 427. Hamburg - 670. Antwerp - 506. Optional Tan/Casablanca - 131. Continental Options - 73. Total = 7402 tons.

Aden was reached at 7am on Thursday 18 May and I gave the Agent the several packages of plans and books for posting. As I had been under the usual pressure to have them ready, it was a relief to deliver them into his care and the hardest part of my job was again over. We discharged cotton piece goods from Kobe, porcelain from Nagoya, cassia and handkerchiefs from Hong Kong and timber from Singapore, into lighters, before sailing at 6pm the same day.

It was 9.15pm on Sunday, 21 May when we arrived off Port Tewfik/Suez.

And, as we had missed the night convoy through the Canal, we anchored to await the morning one. As always, no matter what the time was, the Agent (Wm. Stapledon & Sons) came out to the ship in his launch and the copy of The Egyptian Gazette which he brought me contained the following items of news.

'A thunderous explosion ripped through a string of barges on South Amboy (New Jersey, USA) loaded with ammunition last night (Sat.), killing a possible 29 persons and battering this waterfront city into a tangle of wreckage. Three hundred people, some of them in a critical condition, have been taken to hospitals.' - 'The Chinese Nationalists announced today the abandonment of the Saddle and Parker Islands - small groups near the mouth of the Yangtse.....The withdrawal, accomplished last night, will further cripple the Nationalist blockade of Shanghai.' - 'The Duke of Edinburgh, sailor husband of Princess Elizabeth, was today given his first naval command, - commander of the 1,430-ton frigate, Magpie.' - 'Many women were out early today endeavouring to "get in early" on foodstuffs now point free, as announced last night by the Food Minister, Mr. Maurice Webb. In many places, queues formed outside grocery and provision stores waiting for the doors to open. The biggest demand is for biscuits.' - 'With a Malayan "War Cabinet," and 70.000 troops and police, Britain is reorganising her fight against jungle terrorism in Malaya.' - 'The Leaning Tower of Pisa is slowly but continually falling.' - 'The heated discussion of the moment is that concerning the penalty of the 'cat', which the ignorant claim is too drastic a punishment for this age, but which the learned judges of England wish to see enforced.' - 'Paratrooper John L.R. Rusdell, 18, stood in Court today to hear a death sentence for murdering Mrs. [15]Oilys Scott, 30.' - 'More Arabs are coming into Israel from Egyptian-occupied territory on May 22.....Arab dependents are permitted to enter Israel at varying times under a scheme for the reunion of Arab families.'

At 8.15am the next morning, and with a pilot on board, we weighed anchor to enter the Canal in the northbound convoy. This time, there were no hold-ups, apart from the usual wait in the Bitter Lakes to allow the southbound convoy to exit the northern section, so that we anchored in Port Said harbour exactly twelve hours later. Discharging commenced almost immediately and continued until we sailed at 3.30 in the morning. The cargo discharged consisted of bales of cassia and raw silk from Hong Kong, cases of porcelain from Nagoya (for transhipment to Beirut) and cases of stationery and bags of black pepper from Singapore. And it was

---

[15] As spelt in newspaper.

only after we cleared the port that I could go to bed.

We docked at Tangier at 7pm on Saturday, 27 May. Again discharging began straight away and continued until the cargo of green tea from Taku Bar, tea from Colombo and a case of labels from Hong Kong was out. I was up all night. We sailed at 5.15 in the morning and berthed in Casablanca, at 3 o'clock in the afternoon. And, having discharged green tea from Taku Bar and Hong Kong, we departed for home at 12.30pm on Tuesday 30 May.

When Mike Collyer, our Supernumerary 4th Mate, dropped in for a chat one day, he talked about the necessity to have some kind of hobby to fill in one's free time at sea. I think it was he who told me about a midshipman who had been found unconscious after taking an overdose and had to be marched round the deck to be revived. The sea is not everyone's cup of tea and, with manning so greatly reduced on today's ships, loneliness is now a major problem.

At 5.45am on Friday, 2 June, the Channel pilot boarded at Brixham and brought with him a letter for Captain MacTavish, from a man who was to travel on the ship's next voyage to the Far East. The intending passenger wrote to explain that he would have two dogs with him and when Duncan, who was tired because he had been up all night, dictated a reply to me, he ended it by saying, "Looking forward to seeing you and the dogs." But, catching my glance, he shook his head and smiled as he said to cancel the bit about the dogs! Incidentally, I think it was when nearing home on this voyage that one of our middies developed a head infection. The doctor instructed him to have his head shaved and it was the lad's misfortune to arrive home in this condition. And, in spite of our sympathy, we just couldn't help from laughing at the bald head and protruding ears.

Having changed pilots at Gravesend, we docked in KGV dock at 7am on Saturday the 3rd. The Europeans signed off the same day and Dick went home to Chelsea. I paid off with £17.7.2d (£17.36p); pretty good considering that I had left an allotment of £22 a month. Shortly after we docked, two men were sitting on the settee in my cabin. I don't remember what business they had with me, but one of them was a balding chap in his fifties whom I thought looked rather ignorant until I found out that he spoke fluent Chinese and was Holt's interpreter! And my impression of him was further enhanced when, after inspecting my wages book, he handed it to his companion saying, "Look at that. It's a work of art; far too good for a wages book."!

As Dick had made up his mind to go for his 1st Class PMG, he was not returning to the ship. He studied at the British School of Telegraphy Ltd., 179 Clapham Road, London and, after gaining the Certificate, did only one more foreign voyage with Holts. This was as No.2 on the *Glenearn* (GPGC) and he left the Company because Power, the 1st R/O, made him responsible for the discharge of cargo at one of the Malayan ports and he had no wish to become purser. He then worked for Brocklebanks, Redifon, the Crown Agents, Clan Line, the RFA (Royal Fleet Auxiliary) and Marconi before settling for a shore job in London.

When employed by the Crown Agents, he was on the maiden voyage of the RRS *Shackleton* (GVDC) and, in 1955, when the ship was in the South Atlantic on her way home from Antarctica, I, of all the operators at Portisheadradio, took a telegram from him and sent my salaams. Following that voyage, he was transferred to the RRS *John Biscoe* (MXDS) for her maiden voyage and did a second voyage on her before leaving the Crown Agents. After many years of suffering from osteoporosis and leg ulcers, Dick Molland died, at the age of 81, in the Nuffield Centre in Red Hill on Christmas Eve 2004. He provided me with his reminiscences of the two voyages we made together and retained his remarkable memory of call signs of countless ships and coast stations.

I, too, was not returning as I was bent on having a voyage to Australia before leaving the sea. Some weeks earlier, I had written to ask for this, but, although my request was not immediately granted, and I was left wondering if it would be, it nevertheless established that I was not to sail again on the *Glengarry*. And when I was asked to remain on her for the coasting voyage to the Continent, I was happy to do so.

21   LONDON INTERLUDE

Judith Robles was a Jewish lady in her fifties with whom I had corresponded since we had met briefly in Washington, DC's railway station in 1943. From her home in Brooklyn she had written to say that she was coming to Europe on holiday and we had arranged to meet at the Cumberland Hotel at Marble Arch, where she was staying. I made the journey up to London on the day we docked and, having met Judith and thinking that we were to spend the weekend together, booked in for the night at the same hotel.

Judith, however, had other plans and, during the evening spent at a theatre, she informed me that she was going to see friends the next day. This left me at a loose end and I spent Sunday afternoon at a cinema feeling I had been let down. But I had Judith on board the ship on Wednesday and she subsequently travelled to Dundee to stay with my parents.

John Noble was transferring from the Dundee office of A. & S. Henry & Co. Ltd., where I had worked before going to sea, to their Blackfriars office, as a sales representative. On Monday, 5 June, I again made the journey into town, to meet him coming off the train at Kings Cross. The train was an hour late and it was a very downcast-looking John who emerged from it. He was surprised to see me and said that the Malcolms had done him proud as Eric had seen him off at Dundee. After having something to eat, we went to the Caledonian Christian Club where he was to lodge and to meet his aunt and uncle and their teenage daughter who lived in Palmers Green. But, as I did not find John's relatives friendly towards me and members of the Club affected Scottish accents which they would not have used in Scotland, I was not at all enamoured by the visit.

I spent Saturday, 10 June, with John and this time stayed the night at the Endsleigh Hotel, Endsleigh Gardens near Euston Station, where the bed and breakfast charge of 12/6d was more to my liking. The charge for a single room at the Cumberland was 22/- and the self-service breakfast, 4/3d. The Cumberland, of course, was a much superior hotel. Everything about it was excellent and, unlike the Endsleigh, every room was ensuite. Boot-cleaning, as it was described on the Endsleigh's card, was included in the price of both hotels, but, whereas as the Endsleigh, you were told 'Please bolt your door at night', there were double doors on the rooms at the Cumberland and shoes for cleaning were left between the doors and not in the passage. You did not pay your bill at the Cumberland until you were leaving, but they asked for a deposit of £1:5/- when you booked. A receipt was given for the deposit and although stated on it 'Important:- This Receipt to be presented to Cashier when paying Final Bill', I forgot to do this and forfeited the deposit!

22   SHIPMATES

Captain MacTavish opened the Articles on Friday, 9 June and all but Captain Simpson, who superseded him the next day, and two supernumeraries, who signed before we sailed on the 12th, signed on that day.

The Articles differed from those for our foreign voyages and printed on the front page it said: 'AGREEMENT AND LIST OF THE CREW of a sea-going Home Trade ship having a gross tonnage of 200 tons or more. To be used only for ships employed in trading or going within the following limits:- The United Kingdom, the Channel Islands and Isle of Man, and the Continent of Europe between the River Elbe and Brest inclusive. For this purpose the term "the United Kingdom" is to be construed as including Eire.....This agreement is not to extend beyond the expiration of the period of six months from the date of the agreement.....'

At the top of the page was stamped 'SUPPLEMENTARY TO AN AGREEMENT OPENED ON THE (20.4.50) AT (HONG KONG) FOR A PERIOD NOT EXCEEDING (Two years).' The items in brackets were inserted.

Captain James Simpson was a 50-year-old Scot who had a Master's and not an Extra Master's Certificate as did Captain MacTavish. He was the father of the senior midshipman I had sailed with on the *Atreus* and his home was in Christchurch, Hampshire.

39-year-old R.L. Simon, who had a Master's Certificate, was 1st Mate and his wife, Elizabeth, was one of the supernumeraries. Their home was in Whitley Bay and, strangely enough, while she was listed as his next-of-kin, their son, Michael, was listed as hers. Perhaps she did this in case something happened to both, but her husband was her next-of-kin.

Desmond Stewart and Tao Chi Yuan remained as 2nd and Extra 3rd Mates respectively and we now had no midshipmen.

The uncertificated 3rd Mate, 23-year-old R. Harvey, was married to a Belgian lady and their home address was in Antwerp.

The 2nd Radio Officer, 26-year-old Bernard Kelly, had a 2nd Class PMG and came from Prestwich in Lancashire.

51-year-old W. Thomas was Chief Engineer and had a 1st Class Certificate in Steam and Motor as did 39-year-old A. Knight, the 2nd Engineer.

A. Wishart, the Refrigerating Engineer, was aged 28 and uncertificated.

W.K. Ostle, who had been 4th on the foreign voyage, was now 3rd Engineer and 26-year-old C. Woolmer was 4th.

R. Moffat and L. Kenworthy remained as Assistant Engineers and the other Assistants were D.S. Evans and A.E .Kay, both 23, Stewart D. Nelson, aged 20, and Thomas Michael, aged 21. This was the first voyage of the latter three.

44-year-old S. Buglass was 1st Electrician and 29-year-old I. Lewis, 2nd.

42-year-old H.J. Campbell, from Crieff and who became a friend, was Chief Steward and 46-year-old Assistant Steward A. Linton was his British assistant.

Frederick McCarthy, aged 35, was Supernumerary and, similar to Mrs Simon, was paid at the nominal rate of 1/- a month.

Mr McCarthy and Mrs Simon were really non-paying passengers and we had a further ten passengers who were office staff and spouses, having a holiday at a reduced rate.

Our daily rates of pay were: 1st Mate - £1-16/- : 2nd Mate £1-12/- : 3rd and Extra 3rd Mates - £1-4-8d : 1st Radio Officer (Self) - £1-5-4d : 2nd Radio Officer - 15/8d : Chief Engineer - £2-3-4d : 2nd Engineer - £2 : Refrigerating Engineer - £1-5-4d : 3rd and 4th Engineers - £1-2/- : DS Evans - £1-0-8d : Other Assistant Engineers - £1 : 1st Electrician - £1-12 : 2nd Electrician (on first voyage) - £1-4/- : Chief Steward - £1-5-8d : 2nd Steward - 15/4d. My daily rate worked out at 4d a day more than my basic monthly salary of £38 and I did not receive the purser's bonus of £6 a month when coasting.

23   CONTINENTAL PORTS AND HOME

The cargo for London, our main port of discharge, consisted of rubber, latex, cotton piece goods, aniseed and aniseed oil, cassia and cassia oil, citronella oil, wood oil, mustard oil, teaseed oil, stillingia oil, green tea from China, Ceylon tea, plumbago, timber, hemp, skins, pineapples, goat hair, silk, white pepper, mats, tapioca, palm kernels, hog casings, fibre, canes, seagrass, fish maws, tobacco, rhubarb, firearms, graphite, feathers, sago flour, bristles, stem ginger, ore, cutch (catechu), gum copal, insulation tissue, bamboo poles, desiccated coconut, parasols, vacuum flasks, electric fountains, bush shirts, rubber footwear, torch bulbs, torch cases, personal effects, naval stores, mail and 195 cases of bullion.

As Britain was then a manufacturing nation, making her living by selling her manufactures abroad, her ships, flying the Red Duster, carried the goods abroad and brought back, mainly, the raw materials required to make them. It is a different story today. With her manufacturing base destroyed and her Merchant Navy all but annihilated, the UK is so flooded with foreign goods that it is difficult to find anything British made. Balances of Trade are always unfavourable and it is my belief that, in the long run, financial services alone will not sustain the country.

With discharging complete, we cast off at 12.30pm on Monday, 12 June, 1950 and, from the boat deck, I took a photograph which I have had enlarged and framed. Mr Simon can be seen standing at the bow, near Chinese seamen leaning on the rail and enjoying the view. And the view is something to be admired; the tug at the bow and ocean-going liners on both sides of the dock. The picture also says much for the competence of the Trinity House pilots who could take such a ship through a barge-strewn dock without incident. Those of us who were at sea in those days find it sad and regrettable that such a scene has passed into history.

It was only a short run across the North Sea to Rotterdam. We docked at 1.30 in the morning and later in the day began discharging our cargo of rubber, cotton piece goods, pongee silk, hog casings, apricot and palm kernels, fibre, wood oil, coconut oil (including 136 drums for transhipment to Eire) and Ceylon tea.

This was my first visit to the port and as I was not encumbered with cargo work, I enjoyed it very much. Bent on enjoying their holiday, our passengers were pleasant and, when a coach tour was arranged for them and we were invited to come along, Bernard and I and a couple of others readily accepted. We visited The Hague, Scheveningen, Haarlem and Amsterdam. Lunch was taken at a restaurant in Haarlem and, when I asked for the bill, the waiter said that it had already been settled. Mr Pearce (or it may have been Price), a manager in Holts, was more or less in charge of the party. I found him friendly and played table tennis with him on the boat deck. After four voyages on the ship, this was the first I knew that there was a table on board, but perhaps it was provided for the coastal trip only.

Most of the passengers sat at our table in the saloon and one day the lady next to me asked me to pass the salt. As it was just as near her as it was me, I pointed this out, but she said it was difficult for her to stretch! During the deep-sea voyages, I would have said that the food could not have been bettered. But, no doubt due to the presence of a manager, Mr Campbell gave the lie to this and wine and a cherry were even inserted into a shallow hole cut in the centre of grapefruit.

We sailed at 11.18pm on Sunday, 17 June and docked in Hamburg at 12.36pm the next day to discharge rubber, latex, cotton piece goods, skins, peppermint oil, pongee silk, egg yolk, albumen, coir yarn, sea grass, china grass, goose and duck feathers, goat hair and white pepper. I had had a good time in Hamburg in March, 1946 when on the *Samnesse* and it was pleasant to walk the streets of that lovely city again, with war damage now somewhat less in evidence.

It appeared that we carried a complete cricket set and a group of us went to a grassy area within the docks to have a game. We tossed to form teams. I went into bat first and Kenworthy sent down a fast ball which spread-eagled the wicket. As I hadn't had a bat in my hands for years, I complained that it was unfair that I should be put out by the first ball and said that we should each have a few practice shots first. But, elated by his success, Kenworthy wouldn't hear of it.

When my side were all out, Kenworthy went into bat first for his side. He was a big strong, aggressive, type and, when I bowled the first ball to him, he hit an absolute beauty. But, as it was passing over my head at a rate of knots, I put up my hand, caught it and he, too, was out for a duck. The look of astonishment on his face was delightful to behold and retribution was sweet!
We left at 7.23am on Tuesday, 20 June and Desmond Stewart and Mr Harvey signed off shortly after we docked in Antwerp at 2.24pm on the

21st. Mr Stewart was replaced by E. Kerr, Extra 1st Mate, on the 22nd and P.N. Broad, who had been on the foreign voyage, replaced Mr Harvey on the 23rd. Mr McCarthy, Supernumerary, had left the ship in Rotterdam on the 14th and Mr A.C. Elton, Supernumerary, signed on at the same time at Nick Broad.

As I had visited Brussels twice when on the *Samnesse*, I was not particularly keen on going again, but Mr Campbell persuaded me to accompany him and we had a good day there. At our meal in a restaurant, I remarked on the quality of the meat and Mr Campbell said that, due to its dark colour, he believed it was 'horse'.

At Antwerp, we discharged rubber, hemp, timber, bamboo, hog casings, needles, silk, brushes, wood oil, yang and oak planks, plywood, fibre, pigs' intestines, tea and asparagus. And, as we loaded for the Far East at every port, Voyage 9 of the *Glengarry* had, in essence, begun.

We departed on Saturday, 24 June and docked in KGV again on Sunday. Although we signed off on board that same day, I didn't leave the ship until Wednesday, 28 June, after my relief had arrived. And, as I had first boarded her on 7 January, 1949, I had been on her for almost 18 months.

Because the pink slip issued by the Customs was valid for 'the day of Issue, or on the succeeding day', I had not declared anything when we had returned from the Far East. Now, when I saw the Customs Officer, he questioned me about the binoculars I had bought during the previous foreign voyage and which his colleague had put down as 'second hand'. This man was a different kettle of fish and I had difficulty in persuading him that I had not bought them during the recent voyage.

Apart from the fact that the coasting voyage was enjoyable, I am glad that I did it because it allowed me to complete the round trip of the *Glengarry*. Some thought that I was crazy to give up what was one of the finest ships in the fleet, but the idea of spending my life on, what had begun to seem like, a bus run to the Far East, didn't appeal to me. This, however, was not everyone's point of view as, when R.A. Knight, 1st Radio Officer/Purser was award the MBE in the 1970s, it was stated in the 'Ocean Mail' that he had made 28 consecutive voyages on the *Theseus* between 1955-66 and 15 consecutive voyages on the *Protesilaus* between 1969-72. The *Glengarry* was the only ship on which I did more than one foreign voyage.

The cranes were swinging cargo on board again when I left the ship early on the morning of Wednesday, 28 June, to travel on the 9.40am train from Kings Cross. And when I arrived home shortly after 9pm, my luggage, as usual, contained more than I had gone away with.

It was now a question of waiting to see if I would get that voyage to Australia and during my four weeks' leave, I consulted the Journal of Commerce and Lloyd's List in the Albert Institute Library to see which of Holt's ships were going there. But, as always, this turned out to be a waste of time.

Postscript: The *Glengarry,* which had previously sailed under the names *Meersburg, Hansa* and *Empire Humber*, was to experience yet another name change before being sold to Japanese buyers for scrap in 1970. Earlier that year, Holts had transferred her to the Blue Funnel Line and, re-named *Dardanus*, she sailed from Amsterdam, on the evening of 3 December, for her final voyage to the Far East. During the passage, however, they transferred her back into the Glen Line and she reverted to her original name. But, as there was no time to repaint the funnel, she sailed into Sakkaido with a blue funnel instead of a red one.

24   COASTING THE ELPENOR /GLENFINLAS

After four weeks leave, a letter arrived from Holts on Thursday, 26 July, 1950, instructing me to report to their Liverpool Office at 9am the next day. Eric saw me off on the overnight train from the West Station and, having changed at Perth and Preston, I arrived in Liverpool, at 6.30am on the 28th. I breakfasted at Atlantic House before reporting to Calverley who said I was to coast the *Elpenor* and go straight across to Birkenhead to sign on. But, when I went to do this at the Shipping Office, the Shipping Master refused to let me sign because I did not have my 'ticket' (Certificate of Competency) with me. I had left it in my luggage at the left-luggage office in Lime Street Station and had to trek all the way back to collect and produce it before I was allowed to sign the Articles.

Saturday afternoon was spent in New Brighton with Ken Hancock, the 2nd R/O. Similar to Eric, Ken had completed his National Service as a Tech. Ack (Technical Assistant) in the Royal Artillery and this was his first trip to sea. As we were sailing that evening, we returned to the ship in good time and, shortly after leaving the Vittoria Dock at 8.30pm, Ken informed Seaforthradio (GLV) of the departure of the *Elpenor* (GRQD) for Avonmouth.

Visibility was so poor during the passage that Captain G. McMechan, a friendly man, had me taking D/F bearings both day and night. Although in uniform, Captain McMechan wore slippers and I now wonder if his feet were damaged by frostbite when he spent some time in a lifeboat after the *Dolius* was torpedoed south of Greenland on 5 May, 1943 and when icebergs and pack ice were present.

We docked at Avonmouth at 8.30am on Monday the 31st, a Bank Holiday. Ken and I went into Bristol for the evening and saw a cinema show consisting only of cartoons. The next afternoon, we took a bus to the small town of Shirehampton and very much enjoyed its restful atmosphere. I had previously been in Avonmouth under very different circumstances as, in December, 1944, I had joined the *Samforth* there for a convoyed crossing of the Atlantic to Halifax, NS. And when Michael Shaw and I went to Bristol, the wartime blackout was in force.

On the way into and out of Avonmouth, we could see the town of Portishead, on the Somerset coast, and the transmitting aerials of Portisheadradio. The GPO Radio Station was not, however, located in

Portishead, but at Highbridge. Only the transmitters were at Portishead and were operated from Highbridge.

Burnham-on-Sea Radio (GRL) communicated with ships in the Bristol Channel area on medium wave. We had informed Burnham when entering the port and this was again done when we left it at 8.06pm on Tuesday, 1 August, bound for Rotterdam. I wasn't aware then that Burnhamradio was merely a point within the Portishead Radio Station building at Highbridge and little thought that I would one day work there and live in the pleasant little town of Burnham-on-Sea.

We arrived at the Maas Pilot Boat at 11.45pm on the 3rd and, with a pilot on board, sailed up the 17.4- miles-long Nieuwe Waterweg to dock at 4.12am on the 4th. The Rev. W. Popham Hosford, Chaplain at the Missions to Seamen, boarded later in the day, and I spent the evening at a Mission dance.

The following evening, Ken and I visited the Carnival of Cuba; the funfair section of the 'Rotterdam' - Ahoy Exhibition. One of the sideshows consisted of horses, ridden by visitors, going round in a circle and everyone enjoyed the spectacle of a middle-aged lady struggling to hold down her dress while clinging to her horse. Monday evening was again spent at a Mission dance and, on the afternoon of Wednesday 9 August, we went to the main section of 'Rotterdam Ahoy'.

Rotterdam went through two stages of destruction during the Second World War. The first was on 10 May 1940, when, without declaring war, the Germans invaded the Netherlands and the Luftwaffe reduced the whole of the inner town to rubble in the space of about twenty minutes. (Other cities were spared only because the Government capitulated and for five long years the German treatment of the Dutch was bestial.) The second was in the autumn of 1944 when the retreating Germans systematically destroyed the port before they withdrew.

Assisted by Marshall Aid from the United States, the Dutch had set themselves the target of completing the reconstruction by 1950, and they had succeeded. Rotterdam was now the largest and most up-to-date port on the Continent and the third largest in the world, after London and New York. And the Waalhaven, one of its numerous docks, was the largest artificial basin in the world. Standing on both sides of the River Maas and in its prime position at the estuary of the Rhine, Rotterdam is the Gateway to Europe. By 1959, with oil accounting for half of its trade, it was the largest oil centre in Europe and the next decade saw the building of Europort to cope with expansion.

'Rotterdam – Ahoy' was a celebration of the port's reconstruction which was displayed in model form. It explained how the port was built, reconstructed, operated, and navigation on both the sea and the Rhine. There was also a display of flowers; the country's best-known export and where even the docks had flowerbeds. Only a park separated the Exhibition from the Maas, close to the tunnel which links the northern and southern parts of the town, and although mostly under cover, it extended into the open air. Initially it was to be held from 15 June until 15 August, but, was so successful that it continued into September. We enjoyed the day tremendously, and ended it by again visiting the 'Carnival of Cuba'. To some extent, 'Rotterdam – Ahoy' could be compared with the Festival of Britain, held in London the following year, as both celebrated a return to normality. The entrance charge was f1.50 (f = florin or guilder), but this was reduced to 60 cents for an evening visit. With the rate of exchange f10.64 to £1 sterling, the charges amounted to 2s 10d (14p) and 1s 1½d (5.6p), but for easy calculation we considered the guilder equivalent to the British florin - 2 shillings (10p).

On Thursday, 10 August, the *Elpenor* (7478 grt)) was transferred from the Blue Funnel Line into the Glen Line, renamed *Glenfinlas*, and her blue funnel painted over to become a red one. This was the second time this had happened. From her birth in 1917 until 1935, when Holts had acquired the Glen and Shire Line, she had been the *Elpenor*. In that year, they had transferred her to Glen and Shire and renamed her *Glenfinlas*. And, as she had sailed under that name until 1947, when she returned to the Blue Funnel Line and reverted to her original name, this was a repeat of 1935.

Holts transferred ships between the two lines for taxation purposes and, in 1972, when I took a party of pupils on board the Dutch Blue Funnel ship, *Lycaon*, in Glasgow, I mentioned to her officers that we had sailed into Rotterdam with a blue funnel and come out with a red one. "That's nothing," one said as they all laughed, "You could come out with a yellow one today." The Company had by then acquired Elder Dempster whose ships had a yellow funnel. We were treated to tea on the *Lycaon* that day and, when showing me the Chart Room, Captain van der Voort remarked that, because of shipping congestion, he would rather go into any port other than Rotterdam.

The Missions to Seamen's 'Flying Angel' Clubs were in ports throughout the world and served seamen well. Rotterdam's Flying Angel Club was conveniently situated at Pieter de Hoochweg 133 and the Chaplain boarded every ship which entered the port to invite sailors to use it. If a ship were tied up to buoys, he came out in their launch, *Edith II*, and I know of one occasion when he fell into the water, but which calamity brought only laughter from his assistants and no doubt from the cheerful Popham Hosford himself. By previous arrangement, the *Edith II* collected seamen from these ships at 6.30pm on Sundays, Mondays, Wednesdays and Fridays and returned them at 10.30pm.

The weekly programme of the Club was as follows:

Sunday:	Tea and Social Evening after Service
Monday:	Dance
Tuesday:	Swimming Party
Wednesday:	Whist Drive
Thursday:	English Billiards & Table Tennis
Friday:	Dance
Saturday:	Concert or Whist Drive or Impromptu Evening

A reading room contained the latest newspapers and magazines. There were draughts, chess, cribbage, a radio and a piano. Writing paper and envelopes were provided, you could have a bath or shower, football matches and bus excursions were arranged and services were held in St. Mary's Church, entered by an adjoining door. Food was also available, with hot meals served between 6 and 7pm. Although there was another Mission beside the Wilton-Fijenoord Yard in Schiedam, yet another was being built at Pernis, on the south side of the river where the oil tankers docked.

On Saturday, 11 August, I went to the Club seeking information regarding a tour to Arnhem, prior to going to a cinema to see a 4pm showing of 'The Road to Utopia'; one of the popular 'Road' films in which Bing Crosby, Bob Hope and Dorothy Lamour starred. Unlike in Britain, seats generally had to be booked so that you were given a ticket allocating a particular seat. As this system obtained in many parts of the world, I had come across it before and it was accepted practice to tip the usherette who escorted you to the seat. But it seemed that the practice in the Netherlands was to tip the commissionaire who merely stood beside the desk and provided no service. A seat in the stalls at the Luxor Theatre cost 85 cents (1s 7d); similar to the 1s 9d charged for the same class of seat in a British cinema. As younger people are not familiar with old duodecimal system, I have shown these figures in a more understandable way, but one shilling and nine pence was written as 1/9d.

I returned to the Club for tea and afterwards again met Clare (Klaasje) Mol whom I had danced with the previous evening. I had booked a seat on the tour to Arnhem and, although it was not organised by the Club, I asked her to accompany me. She hesitated to accept the invitation, but the girls standing beside us persuaded her and she did.

The tour left from Lindeman Square at 9am, but I was there by 8.15 because I was anxious to get a seat for Clare. She arrived a few minutes before the coach set off and all but myself were Dutch.

My reason for choosing the tour was to visit the British Airborne Cemetery (Airborne Kerkhof) at Oosterbeek, near Arnhem, and when I had booked it, I was assured that we would be going there. This information, however, proved incorrect. It was a Mystery Tour and if Clare hadn't made the driver aware of what I had been told, he wouldn't have stopped at Oosterbeek. When the coach drew up at the cemetery gates, I was astonished to find that when Clare and I descended from it, all the others remained seated.

Operation 'Market Garden', begun on 17 September, 1944, was the name given to the largest single airborne operation of the war. Its aim was to capture three bridges over the Rhine and, although the 1st Airborne Division initially succeeded in their objective, they met fierce resistance and were slaughtered. It was raining slightly as we walked between the rows of graves of the hundreds, if not thousands, of young men who lie there. The cemetery is beautifully kept, with flowers between the graves over which are white-painted metal crosses giving name, rank and exact date of death, if known - 'Sgt. J McKnight, 1. Para. Regt. 20.9.44' : 'S/Sgt. W. Goodwin, Glider P. Regt. Sept. 1944' : 'Sgt. J. Johnstone, Glider P. Regt. 9.44' : etc. etc. Some of the crosses bear only the word UNKNOWN while over the grave of Sgt. T.A. Klagenstein, A A C, 9.44, is the Star of David. There are many such cemeteries throughout Europe and once, when I took a party of pupils to see a First World War cemetery in Northern France, many of them too didn't get off the bus.

Having made a brief stop in Haarlem, the coach drew up outside the Hotel Pension De Dennen in Renswoude for lunch. But nobody went in as all, including Clare, had brought sandwiches. Among other places visited, was the Hotel De Wereld (The World) in Wageningen where the occupying German forces had signed the capitulation agreement. Due to its significance, the hotel had been left unaltered and a metal plate at the entrance commemorated the event. Clare was an excellent interpreter and when the others showed interest in something I didn't comprehend, she explained that we were going up a hill. It is common knowledge that the Netherlands is a flat country, but, as we were negotiating only a slight gradient, this brought it home to me.

I was to meet Clare again on a future visit to Rotterdam and correspond with her for over forty years. A year or two later, she told me that, during an overnight ferry crossing to England, she had found herself sharing a cabin with a German lady. The lady tried to be friendly, but, although a very religious and kind person, Clare refused to talk to her. And, when she sent me a copy of 'Verwoesting en Wederopbouw' (Revival In The Netherlands) and I saw the awful pictures it contains, I understood why.

We sailed at 12.15pm on Saturday, 19 August. We had notified Scheveningen Radio Station (PCH) when entering the port and now told them of our departure for London.

As we neared KGV the following day, an ex-R/O office bod boarded from a launch to collect my wages book. I stood at the rail to meet him and his first words were, "Where did you pick this one up?" He was referring to the ship and the rail on which I leaned was worn thin in parts with age. Northforelandradio (GNF) was informed of our arrival and after we docked at 7pm, Ken I went into North Woolwich for the evening.

My father was in Eastbourne on business and I was able to spend Friday with him when he was on his way back to Dundee. Because of this, and because both John Noble and David Logan were in London, I booked in for the Friday and Saturday nights at the central Endsleigh Hotel rather than make the long journeys from and to the ship.

On Saturday afternoon, John and I went to the Kennington Oval to see Surrey playing Lancashire where such illustrious figures as Washbrook and Edrich played for Lancashire and Laker and Bedser for Surrey. But we got soaked in a torrential rain shower and I had to borrow John's best suit to go to the dance in the Hampstead Town Hall.

David also attended the dance and, when the three of us were standing beside Big Ben the next day, he provocatively asked a young policeman for the time. But the policeman didn't fall for it and pointed to the clock. The remainder of the day was spent at Epping where we had both lunch and tea in one of those pleasant tearooms which no longer exist. As I was returning to the ship, I left the others when the train back to the City arrived at Mile End. Another train took me to Plaistow where I caught a bus to Silvertown and the docks.

Captain Power, an elderly retired master whose duties were more akin to those of a watchman, was standing by the ship. He was pleasant enough and, although I knew that I should have asked his permission to go off for the weekend, I had chosen not to do so because I suspected that he might not have allowed me to go. When I returned to the ship, he told me that he had informed the Marine Superintendent, Captain Baxter Jones, of my absence and that I was to report to him at the dock office on Monday morning.

During the telling-off I received from Baxter Jones, he asked the name of my last ship. I think that, as I was on the old *Glenfinlas*, he expected me to name another old ship before saying that, if I continued with such behaviour, I had little chance of promotion to a better ship. When I replied, "The *Glengarry*, he gave a muffled grunt and told me to apologise to Captain Power which I did. Although the reprimand was not anticipated, I felt no rancour. I knew it was justified and was well pleased with my fait accompli.

We had already signed off the Articles and, when my relief arrived the next morning, Tuesday, 29 August, I was amazed to find that he had brought his own filing cabinet with him. Goodness knows what he carried in it and just imagine lugging a steel filing cabinet, in addition to your luggage, to and from every ship. Perhaps he was new to the purser game, but I thought that, if he continued with this practice, he would certainly make a name for himself in the Company!

I left the ship that afternoon and, as it had been only a coasting trip, I was travelling light with only a suitcase and a grip. Because of this, I didn't see why I should give the Port of London Authority policeman at the dock gate the usual half-crown bribe to prevent him ransacking my luggage to see if I were bringing in more dutiable goods than those mentioned on my customs slip. To my delight, he behaved true to form and I enjoyed standing by the taxi as he searched through my things before allowing me through. And, because I had not supplied the bribe, this was the one and only time my luggage was examined.

After dumping my suitcase at the Left Luggage Office in the station, I spent the evening with John. The queue which we joined at the Leicester Square Theatre was entertained by buskers and the film, "Destination Moon", was pure science fiction as it was nineteen years later before man set foot on the planet. After supper at Lyon's Corner House in Piccadilly and collecting a shirt I had left at the Caledonian Christian Club, where John lodged, I walked back to spend another night at the Endsleigh.

On the train to Liverpool in the forenoon, I found myself in the company of R.A. Knight, the 1st RO/Purser previously mentioned. At India Buildings, Calverley told me I could go home on leave and, when booking a room at Atlantic House, I met an AB from the *Glenfinlas* and we went to the pictures together. My train left the next morning and, when I arrived home that evening, I had been away for thirty-five days.

Postscript: Having been built on the Tyne by Hawthorne, Leslie in 1917 and serving the Company well during her long and adventurous life, the *Elpenor/Glenfinlas* transmitted her final message to Cullercoatsradio (GCC) on 10 June, 1952 - "Glenfinlas QTP (entering) Blyth (Northumberland) for breaking up (for scrap) CL (closing the station)". Even in death, old ships prove useful.

25 COASTING THE HELENUS

At about 7pm on Wednesday 6 September, a telegram arrived from Holts telling me that I was to coast the *Helenus* and to report at the Glasgow Marine Superintendent's office before 5pm the next day.

The train left Dundee at 1pm and I descended from it at Stirling where I had to change. As there was a wait between trains, I went into the buffet for a cup of tea and, when I bent to pick up my suitcase, something happened to my back so it was with difficulty that I boarded the train. On the way out to KGV in Shieldhall, I had the taxi driver stop at a chemist where I bought a tube of liniment.

At breakfast the next morning, I sat beside the man I was relieving. He was an older man and, on learning that I came from Dundee, he said that, before the war, he had served on DP & L (Dundee, Perth and London) ships sailing between Dundee and London. This reminded me of standing on the dock with my parents as a DP & L ship arrived from London. With all the passengers on deck and so many people on the quay as the ship moved slowly towards its berth, it seemed a big occasion when I was perhaps ten and London a far-off place.

Together with Mr Eynon, the 2nd Mate, I signed on the Articles at the Shipping Office in the forenoon, but had no idea that the 2nd Mate he was relieving was Ian Smith until I stepped into the chart room and found him there. Ian had been 3rd Mate on the *Samite* when I was a first-trip 3rd Sparks and, although we were never friends, we had spent many evenings together during that fifteen-month voyage playing monopoly in the 4th Engineer's cabin. He grinned in recognition, but we had no conversation.

As there was no master on board, I went to the Dock Office to ask Captain Skinns, the Marine Super, if I might go home for the weekend and, having obtained his permission, I travelled back to Dundee in the late afternoon.

I was walking only with difficulty and, as Dr Fraser lived quite near us, I went to see him about my back. Mrs Fraser answered the door and, although I explained that I was in pain and doubted I would be able to rejoin the ship, she said there were no consultations that evening and that I couldn't see her husband. I could hear that they had friends in, but was so anxious that I continued to remonstrate with her and, hearing the dispute, Dr Fraser came to see what it was all about. When I explained the situation to him, he told me to come into the surgery where he examined me, said that I had strained a back muscle and gave me a note stating that it was unlikely that I would be able to rejoin the ship.

I was more relieved to have the note than to have the complaint diagnosed. It covered me if I were unable to rejoin, but I never used it as I was sufficiently recovered the next day to go to the YMCA Grounds with Eric, and to the Palais in the evening.

When travelling back to Glasgow on Sunday evening, I got talking to the girl sitting opposite me in the compartment. "What's the name of your ship?" she asked. When I replied that it was the *Helenus*, she said, "That's my name. Helen." Blue Funnel Line ships were named after the mythical Greek heroes and Helenus was not a woman, but a son of Priam, King of Troy, and a brother of Hector.

On Monday morning, I 'phoned Marie Crabb and arranged to meet her when she finished work. We had tea at the nearby Ivy Restaurant before going to Cranston's Cinema and, after seeing her home, I got back to the ship about 10.40pm.

Built in 1949, the *Helenus* (GBTM), was the first of Holt's four beautiful 'H' Class ships. Similar to the *Hector* (1950) and the *Ixion* (1951), she was built at the Harland & Wolff Yard in Belfast while the *Jason* (1950) came from the Swan, Hunter Yard at Wallsend-on-Tyne. Designed for the Australian trade, they were single-screw steam-turbined ships of 10125 gross registered tons with an average speed of 18 knots and had accommodation for twenty-nine first-class passengers.

With Captain Coates, who was to remain on the ship for the deep-sea voyage, now on board, we sailed at 1.44pm on Thursday, 14 September and C. Branthwaite, the 2nd R/O, notified Portpatrickradio (GPK) of our departure for Liverpool. We were in the Mersey by 3am and, when berthed in Birkenhead that morning, the breakfast menu read:

*AH House Flag   *s.s. "HELENUS"   September 15th

BREAKFAST

Oatmeal   Porridge
Boiled   Manx   Kipper
Grilled   Empire   Bacon
Fried   &   Turned   Eggs
Light   Cakes -   Syrup
Preserves
Tea   Coffee

*Embossed

We signed off the Articles and, when I crossed to India Buildings to see where I was to go next, Calverley said it would be either Glasgow or London, but to come back the following day. On my way back to the ship, I called at the Dock Office where I met Midshipmen Dugald McNab and Gordon Henderson who had been on the *Glengarry* during my second voyage on her. Another middy was with them and the four of us went to the pictures together.

After spending another night on the *Helenus*, I returned to India Buildings to be told by Calverley that it was to be Glasgow, but that I could go home meantime and be back in Liverpool by 9am next Wednesday. I was taken aback by this. I had been home enough recently and, when I pointed this out, it was his turn to be surprised. Fancy anyone complaining about having too much leave! But it was the thought of the long rail journeys for a couple of days at home that really bothered me.

Gerry Davies had been Extra 3rd/4th Mate during two of my voyages on the *Glengarry* and, when I fortuitously met him in the Officers' Waiting Room, I collected the money he owed me for taking his camphor-wood chest through Customs. We had lunch together before I caught the 2.15pm north. For part of the journey, I travelled with two chaps from the *Troilus* and, when the train arrived in Dundee, I found Eric had foregone a Saturday evening at the Palais to meet me. He had had a long wait; it was 11.06pm and the train should have arrived at 10.15.

26   COASTING THE PATROCLUS

On the evening of Tuesday, 19 September, 1950, my mother saw me off on the overnight train to Liverpool. The Korean War was on and, on the platform, we met an ex-regular who had been recalled from the reserve. There were the usual changes at Perth and Preston and when I arrived in Liverpool at 6.30am, I made for Atlantic House to have a shave and breakfast before going to India Buildings.

After Calverley had told me that I was to coast the *Patroclus* (GMSL) to Glasgow, I left to join her and sign on the Articles in Birkenhead. Captain Alderton was the coasting skipper and Alan Baker, making his first trip, was my No.2.

We sailed at 6.30am on Friday the 22nd and, when the Clyde pilot boarded off the Little Cumbrae in the evening, he brought with him a Clyde Port Authority form which I was given to complete. As the form referred only to vessels coming from abroad, I went up to the bridge to see him, but he said that all incoming ships were required to complete the form and laughed as he added that England *was* a foreign country!

As we proceeded up the estuary, we caught up with the *Bellerophon*, but instead of passing her as we could easily have done, Alderton reduced speed to follow her in. The reason for this was that he knew that Lawrence Holt and other seniors of the Company were on board and felt it would be disrespectful to pass! About to set out on her maiden voyage, the *Bellerophon* (7707 grt) had come round the north of Scotland from the Caledon Shipyard, partly owned by Holts, in Dundee. She was the twelfth of Holt's 'A' ships built between 1947 and 1950 and a further fifteen were to be built between 1951 and 1958. Motor ships with an average speed of 15 knots, they had accommodation for twelve passengers and became Holt's workhorses in the Far East.

The *Patroclus* (10109 grt) was one of the four 'P' Class ships. Similar to the 'H' Class, they had steam-turbine engines, averaged 18 knots and had accommodation for twenty-nine passengers, but, as they were built for the Far East and not the Australian trade, did not have as much refrigerated space. On their monthly service from Birkenhead, they called only at Rotterdam before travelling non-stop to Singapore in only twenty days, thus re-establishing Blue Funnel's pre-war claim of providing the fastest cargo service to the Far East. When I took a picture of the *Patroclus* in

KGV Dock, in line behind her were the *Bellerophon*, the *King David* (an Elder Dempster ship) and the Liberty Ship *Titan* (ex-Samgara). See page 86.

Many office staff still worked Saturday mornings, but, when I 'phoned Marie's office and there was no reply, I called at her house in Harrison Drive. There was nobody in and, when a letter arrived on Wednesday, it explained that she and her brother had spent the weekend in the Borders with a church group. I 'phoned her at the office and we again had tea at the Ivy before going to the pictures as we had done two weeks earlier.

On Friday afternoon, and as Captain Alderton was not on board, I went to the Dock Office to ask Captain Skinns if I might go home for the weekend. He wasn't in, but a clerk had told him that someone wanted to see him so that when he stepped from the gangway and I approached him, he put two and two together and said "Oh, it's you again." He appeared to be in a bad mood and, when I made my request, replied "No, you bloody well can't." I smiled and said, "Thank you very much, sir", but, as I was mounting the stairs into the accommodation, he called out after me "Can you be back by Sunday evening?" I have always remembered that interview. It pays to be civil.

Captain Skinns retired and was succeeded by Captain AJ Kent in 1957. When the latter retired in 1973, the Dock Office was closed and ships berthed in Glasgow were thereafter kept fully manned. Roxburgh, Colin Scott & Co., owned by Holts, were our Agents and, when a number of men had to be paid off from either the *Patroclus* or the *Helenus*, one of their clerks insisted that it was my job to make up their wage accounts. I was too long in the tooth to be taken in by this and he did the job at my insistence.

When I 'phoned Marie on Monday forenoon to let her know that we were sailing that evening, she said that my parents had 'phoned earlier to say they were coming through to Glasgow for the day and that they were to have tea with her at the Ivy. I knew that my father had the day off because it was the Dundee Fast, but, as they had said nothing of this to me when I was home for the weekend, it was obviously a last minute decision. When I joined them at the Ivy, my parents said that they would like to see over the ship, but, as the Marine Superintendent's party would be making their inspection before we sailed, I put them off the idea. Marie and I saw them off on the Dundee train at 7pm and when I returned to the ship after supper at her house, it was to find that the inspection had been cancelled. I have always regretted not showing my parents over the *Patroclus* that day. They never saw any of the ships I was on and, even if they had been on board during an inspection, I don't suppose it would have mattered.

We sailed at around midnight, docked in Birkenhead in the morning and after signing off at 2.30pm, I crossed on the ferry to Liverpool to report at India Buildings for further instructions from Calverley. This time, there was no delay. The *Medon* was also in Birkenhead and I was to coast her to the Continent.

Postscript: The *Helenus* was sold to ship breakers in Kaohsiung, Taiwan in 1973 and the *Patroclus* went the same way the following year. In 1977, the *Bellerophon* was sold to the Saudi-Europe Line of Jeddah for further trading.

27   COASTING THE MEDON

I returned to Birkenhead to sign on the *Medon* at the Shipping Office where I stood among the others while the Shipping Master rapidly read the conditions of service on the Articles before we signed them. I then transferred my gear from the *Patroclus* to the *Medon*, had dinner and remained on board.

We sailed at 4.30pm the next day; Wednesday, 4 October, 1950. Captain W. Stanger was Master and my No.2, J. Finbar (Barry) O'Keeffe, an Irishman, was again a first-tripper with a 2nd Class ticket. Barry told me that he had worked for a spell on the ship-to-shore radio station at Cobh, near Cork, in the Republic of Ireland; a station I had never heard of. And the first message he sent from the ship was "GLV (Seaforthradio) de (from) GOFR (our call sign) QTO (leaving) Birkenhead bnd Amsterdam".

Originally the *Empire Splendour*, the *Medon* (7368 grt), a 12-knot single-screw motor ship, had been built in the Belfast Yard of Harland & Wolff in 1942 for the Ministry of War Transport. Holts had managed her from the outset and renamed her when they bought her in 1946.

Having passed through the North Sea Canal, we arrived in Amsterdam on Sunday, 8 October. And, the following morning, when a launch took me to the Dutch Blue Funnel office of the Nederlandsche Stoomvaart Maatschappij Oceaan M.V. at Prins Hendrik Kade 159, I admired the fine buildings we passed and thought how pleasant it was to travel in this way. Although, courtesy of our passengers, I had already visited the city in June when the *Glengarry* was in Rotterdam, we hadn't a great deal of time then and I now made the most of it.

Because it had not been subjected to the bombing received by Rotterdam, all the old buildings remained intact and it was a treat just to wander through the streets and beside the many canals which divide the city into ninety islands. I made a tour of the canals and harbour on one of G.A.Meijer's luxury launches which left every 15 minutes from the Damrak and where the guide's commentary was in Dutch, English, German and French. On visiting the Rijksmuseum, the National Gallery, I had to leave my camera at the entrance before viewing the paintings of such Dutch artists as Rembrandt, Hals, Rubens, Vermeer and Pieter de Hoogh and where the prize exhibit is Rembrandt's 'Nachtwacht' (Night Watch). Rembrandt was a native of Amsterdam and I went to see his house, now a museum, only to find that it was after 5pm, when it closed. The entrance charge at the Rijksmuseum was 10 cents (2½d or about 1p).

Armed with an official weekly programme which I obtained at the British Consulate and which contained a plan, I generally preferred to walk everywhere although single-deck trams were cheap and plentiful. The fare to any destination was 11 cents and if you required to change trams, you could do so within 45 minutes at no extra charge. A thing which struck me about the trams was that they carried post boxes and I saw a man running up to a tram just to post a letter.

As I was walking through the dock area one afternoon, a man in a group of workers shouted something to me. I didn't, of course, understand and when he saw this, he pointed to his wrist. I then called out "Four o'clock" and he shouted back "Vier uur, dank U veel". Some yards farther on, another workman shouted to me and, although again I didn't understand, I called back "Vier uur" and he too thanked me!

On Sunday, 15 October, Barry and I went on a Noord-Zuid-Hollandsche Vervoermaatschappij N.V Special Winter tram and boat tour, costing f 1.95 (less than 4/- or 20p), to Volendam and Marken on the IJsselmeer. Although called a tour, it was merely an open ticket as you could leave at any time between 8.40am and 4pm, return at any time between 1.15pm and 7.55pm, take trams as you please and spend as long as you liked at the places. Also, there was no guide and we travelled independently. As the ship was berthed on the opposite side of the harbour from the Central Station, where the tour began, we crossed over by launch. The tram then brought us back to our side of the harbour and ran past the ship on its 55-minute journey to Volendam via Monnikendam and Edam.

One of the attractions of both Volendam and Marken was that the people still wore traditional dress. We spent some time in Volendam and had lunch at the Hotel van Diepen where, including one bier and a service charge, it cost a total of f7.10 (14/- or 70p). We then went by tram to Monnikendam from where a small boat took us over to the island of Marken. The headdress of the Marken women was different from that of Volendam and they wore their hair longer. Also, young boys and girls looked exactly the same as they too had long hair and wore identical dress until about the age of seven. There were Dutch, Belgian, USA and Canadian visitors, but, although both towns profited from tourism, they still engaged in fishing and, in the early evening at Marken, we stood beside the women and children watching the boats set out. After recrossing to Monnikendam, we returned to Amsterdam by tram. Incidentally, I am convinced that the people of Volendam and Marken did not continue to wear the old form of dress merely to attract tourists and was later surprised to hear Clare say that the other Dutch felt somewhat ashamed of them. At any rate I found them happy and friendly and very willing to be photographed.

Volendam, Marken, Monnikendam and Amsterdam itself were all on the Zuyder Zee until 1929 when the 18½-mile-long Afsluitdijk, connecting North Holland and Friesland, was completed to shut it off from the North Sea. The enclosed area was then drained to rid it of salt water in order to create polderland and, fed by rivers, the fresh water IJsselmeer. Ocean-going ships proceeding to and from Amsterdam were not affected as, due to the silting up of the Zuyder Zee and the fear that its entrance might become blocked, the Noordzee Kanaal, linking the port to the North Sea at Ijmuiden, had been completed in 1876. Until I visited the Netherlands, I had no idea of the size of the dykes. Built to withstand the remorseless pounding of the sea, they carry roads, buildings and trees. The road over the Afsluitdijk is 300 yards wide and two-fifths of the Netherlands is below sea level. As a canal connects Amsterdam to the Rhine, many of the barges which ply the river are always to be seen in both Amsterdam and Rotterdam. Some go as far as Basle in Switzerland while others serve the Ruhr and, as they are also homes, colourful curtains at the windows/portholes display the woman's touch. When the German forces were withdrawing in 1944, not only did they destroy the port of Rotterdam, but they also opened the dykes to flood the land it had taken years to reclaim.

Stefan Askenase was giving one-night Chopin piano recitals in twelve cities of the Netherlands. On Monday evening Barry and I went to hear him in the large hall of the Concertgebouw where he was so appreciated that he played three extra pieces.

We sailed for Rotterdam the next day and as we exited the lock at IJmuiden and saw a boatload of women being thrown about in the rough sea, I thought what a hardy lot they were.

I 'phoned Clare on arrival in Rotterdam on Wednesday, 18 October and Peter, the 4th Mate, and I took her and her friend Nellie to the pictures at night. Nellie, a very slim girl who also attended the Mission, was engaged to a Geordie sailor and later came to live in England.

The Mission again became the centre of my social life and, when Popham Hosford came over one day to see who was tinkering at the piano, he said, "Oh, it's you again."! Miss L.O. Gellatly was the Lady Warden and, when she was later travelling home to Aberdeen on leave, it was a coincidence that she sat beside my father on the train.

As the following menu shows, the food on the *Medon* was up to the usual standard.

MV "MEDON"   20th October 1950

(Drawing of ship with THE BLUE FUNNEL LINE printed in a scroll below)

MENU

DINNER

Pea Soup Natural
Poached Turbot. Tomato Sauce.
Roast Gosling. Savoury Sauce.
Roast & Boiled Potatoes.
Green Peas.
Coconut Pudding.
Cheese.   Biscuits.
Coffee.

Although I walked through the Maas Tunnel several times, I never made the mistake which Eric made a few years later when, somehow or other, he missed the walkway. It was almost 5 o'clock when he entered the 1.16-mile-long yellow-tiled tunnel and all was quiet until cyclists, coming from the other side, suddenly began to whiz past and call out to him. It was only then that he realized that he had taken the wrong path, but as hundreds of cyclists were passing him at speed, he felt it too dangerous to turn back and, keeping as close to the side as he could, continued to the end. There are so many cyclists in the Netherlands that, outside town centres, there is often a cycle path between the pavement and the road. And, when I forgot this, I was sometimes reminded by a cyclist nearly hitting me. The bikes appear to have no brakes, but braking it achieved by back-peddling.

On Sunday, the 22nd, I went on another trip with Clare. We met at the Delft's Poort Railway Station at about 9.30am and bought tickets to The Hague. These allowed us to break the journey at Delft, ten miles away, so that we got off to spend an hour or so in that picturesque little town, famous for its blue china and where Vermeer had painted. After seeing the Old Church and the building where William of Orange had once stayed, now a museum, we were crossing the small bridge when a lady said to me "Is dat het oude kerk, meneer?" It was so like Scots that I knew what she said, but left it to Clare to answer.

It was only five miles to The Hague and, after lunch at the Hotel Hof van Holland, we visited Mesdag's Panorama; a most unusual painting of a beach scene at nearby Scheveningen. Mesdag, with the assistance of his wife, set up a circular piece of glass on the beach and, standing inside it, they painted the scene on to it. It was then taken to the circular room of the house, a light placed inside it projected the scene onto the wall and he painted it. Sand placed on the floor beneath the 14 x 36m painting, blended in with it to create such a sense of realism that the snapshot I took has the appearance of being taken on the beach itself. The toegang/entrance charge was f 0.15 (3½d or 1½p).

On leaving the Panorama, we went on a tour of the Gevangenpoort (Prison Gate) where the entrance charge was f 0.25 (6d or 2½p). The guide spoke only in Dutch and, when we were in Cornelis de Witt's Room and Clare was translating for me, she was told to shush!

Our next stop was at the Houses of Parliament and the 13th-century Gothic Ridderzaal or Hall of the Knights, in the ancient inner court of the Binnenhof and where the Queen opens a new session of Parliament with her speech from the Throne. We then walked to the Peace Palace, the seat of the International Court of Justice, but didn't have time to go in as I wanted to see Scheveningen. The Peace Palace, completed in 1913, was built with $1,500,000 donated by Andrew Carnegie, the Scottish, Dunfermline-born, philanthropist who made his millions in the USA. Prior to the building of the Peace Palace, the International Court had no permanent residence. In addition to financing the building of the Peace Palace, Carnegie provided the library it contains and, in recognition of his generosity, the Carnegieplein was named in his honour.

During the 1½-mile tram ride to Scheveningen, Clare provocatively left it to me to pronounce the name to the conductor when buying the tickets. Although Scots, used to guttural sounds, can make a good stab at it, only the Dutch can pronounce it properly. During the German occupation, the Dutch tested to see if a person were really Dutch, and not a German claiming to be Dutch, by getting him or her to say Scheveningen.

On arriving in the centre of the town, we walked back along the wide promenade towards The Hague and saw the spot where Mesdag painted his panorama before having afternoon tea in a clean little shop in the main street. It was time to go back now and, while we were waiting for a tram to The Hague, a young lad hit me on the head with a stick. And, when I promptly clouted him, I received a stream of abuse from his sister. After the 15-mile train journey back to Rotterdam, we had a meal in a Chinese Indies restaurant. Clare then pleaded with me to attend the service at the Mission Church, but, although I should have gone to please her, I stubbornly refused and saw her onto her bus before heading back to the ship.

I cannot now say whether it was during this or my previous visit to Rotterdam that the following amusing incident occurred, but it was related to me the following day by the young mate involved. Having met and spent money on a girl in a nightclub, he was to stay the night with her in her flat. They went by taxi and, when she told the driver to stop, she informed the young man that her flat was round the corner, but that she didn't want the taxi to stop in front of it as it might attract the attention of the neighbours. She then went off by herself and, after adhering to her instructions to wait several minutes, he went round the corner and, finding the entry door locked and not knowing which flat she occupied, he roused the whole tenement in his attempts to locate her. And, of course, he never saw her again!

We sailed for Hamburg on Wednesday, 25 October and, when I took a form to Captain Stanger, which had something to do with currency and required his signature, he said that he wasn't going to be dictated to by any Germans. But, when I pointed out that Hamburg was under British Military control, he reluctantly signed. Captain Stanger's quarters were directly at the bottom of the stairs which led to my cabin. He was a tall strong-looking irascible man and at the beginning of the trip when I had my radio on rather loud, one of the mates advised me to turn it down. During the previous voyage, Stanger had silenced an offending radio by putting his fist through it!

It was always a pleasure to sail up the Elbe to Hamburg where we docked on the morning of the 27th. During a visit to the shops, I came across folding umbrellas for the first time and, thinking this a great idea, bought one for my mother. We sailed again, for Liverpool, on Sunday, the 29th.

I had an office on the *Medon*. It was on the port side of the main deck and, when I was sitting at my desk on Tuesday afternoon, the ship was rolling in a calm sea so that, when it rolled to port, I could see the sea through the porthole. Suddenly I saw a line of drift nets and by the time I had run out on deck, we had ploughed straight through them. It was Blue Funnel practice to keep a double watch on the bridge when vessels were coasting, but as Michael Campbell, the 3rd Mate, was there by himself, he was fully responsible. Stanger, an Orkney man and no doubt of fishing stock, gave Michael hell and refused to sign his watch-keeping certificate to allow him to sit for his 2nd Mate's ticket. We were in the Dogger Bank area and I cannot understand why Michael didn't see the nets on such a clear day. It was, however, a salutary lesson for him and the Liverpool Office later persuaded Stanger to sign his certificate.

Another less serious incident occurred during that trip. There was an adjoining door into the wireless room from my cabin and I heard a Blue Funnel ship calling us when Barry was on watch one evening. I waited for him to reply, but when the ship called again and he still didn't, I went through and said, "Aren't you going to answer him?" Barry was flustered; he was reading a book and hadn't heard our call sign. Afterwards he said to me, "I'll never read on watch again." He would and I often did, but the first thing I did on joining a new ship was to memorize her call sign so that it became imprinted in my mind.

We docked in Birkenhead on Thursday, 2 November and signed off the next day. I paid duty on only the umbrella which the Customs Officer generously valued at 15/- (75p) and charged me 12/- (60p). I was told I could go home on leave and when I arrived in Dundee on Friday evening, and ignoring my weekend home from the *Patroclus* in Glasgow, I had been away for a month and a half.

Postscript: Holts sold the *Medon* in 1963 and, renamed the *Tina*, she sailed under the Liberian flag until broken up in China in 1970.

28   LOOKING FOR A SHIP

On Wednesday, 8 November, 1950, a telegram arrived from Holts instructing me to report to the Marine Superintendent in London before 5pm the next day. But, as this meant that I would have to take the night train, I decided to take a chance and leave in the morning. Eric saw me off and I 'phoned John when the train pulled in at King Cross about 4pm.

As it was after 5 o'clock when I reached the Dock Office at KGV, work in the docks was over for the day and it was closed. As I had no idea which ship I was to join, this presented a problem and, carrying my suitcase and grip, I began walking down the long dock looking for red or blue funnels. A glance at the shipping newspapers in the Central Library in Dundee, had led me to suspect that I might be joining the *Radnorshire*, but there was no sign of her and I later learnt that she had sailed for the Continent on Monday. KGV was a very long dock and I was tired and anxious when I spotted the *Glengarry* at her usual berth, on the opposite side to where I was. I walked round the head of the dock and, as I was approaching her, a number of her Chinese crew who were heading for the town, greeted me like an old friend. And, when I boarded her, it was with relief that I found that I was expected and was to standby her until the *Clytoneus* came in. Because I had turned up late, I thought that I might have the pleasure of another talking-to from Baxter Jones, but, as I heard nothing from him, felt pleased that my gamble, although tarnished by the anxiety I had experienced, had come off.

I had developed a sore throat on the train south and, by Friday morning, the cold had gone into my chest and I could barely speak. I cannot now be certain, but believe that Dr Moloney was again the ship's surgeon and he gave me tablets to dissolve in water, and told me to gargle without saying what they were. When I gargled and realized they were only salt tablets and complained of this to him, he replied that there was nothing better for a sore throat.

John came down to the ship in the evening. It was raining cats and dogs so that he said, "There's only one person I would do this for Malcolm and that's me."! I didn't have a pass for him to stay the night, but, when he elected to bed down on my settee, I, with my heavy cold, said that, if he didn't already have a cold, I could guarantee that he'd have one by morning. I had been applying and consuming Vick all day and, when I got him to rub my back, he said it was a miracle that my cold was managing to survive!

When I wakened John shortly after Chu Ching Fah had come in for the supper tray, he noticed that the door curtain was not drawn, as it had been the previous evening, and asked if I had been out during the night. And, when I told him the steward had been in, he said, "If that guy is intelligent, he'd notice that there's two of us here and bring two cups of tea." I had not told the steward not to bring morning tea as I normally did and, although I didn't credit Chu with such intelligence, he did bring two cups and I let John have both. He was shaving when I returned from breakfast and when, because he thought I had been away a long time, he asked where I had been, I told him that, as I didn't want to keep him waiting too long, I had rushed through breakfast and all I had was ....! When I left him at the dock gate, he said, "Fancy - no breakfast!" and that a letter of complaint would be going to my parents!

I had met Helen Macpherson at the Dundee Palais on 21 April, 1947 - the day before her 20th birthday and six days before my 22nd. Shortly after we met, she had entered the civil service as a shorthand typist in the Board of Trade office in Glasgow and I had gone to study for my 1st Class ticket at Leith Nautical College. But, we had broken up a couple of days before Christmas, 1947 and, although I had recovered from the deep hurt experienced, I had never really got her out of my system and I decided to try to renew the relationship. Helen was now a Personal Assistant/Clerical Officer/Secretary to an Assistant Secretary at Board of Trade Headquarters in Millbank in London. During my leave after my final voyage on the *Glengarry*, I had written to her at the Millbank address and, as a favourable reply was received, our relationship was renewed. But, due to having been in Geneva with her boss, she had not been in London during my previous visit.

Helen and I had arranged to meet outside Lyon's Corner House in the Strand at 2 o'clock on Saturday. I left the ship in good time, but, on arrival at the dock gate, the Port of London Authority policeman wouldn't allow me through because I didn't have a pass for my camera. As I had bought it second-hand four years previously, it was, and looked, an old one, but although I pointed this out, he remained adamant. And, because I had to return to the ship to get the pass, I was late for our first meeting in three years.

After lunch at a somewhat expensive restaurant near Piccadilly and walking to the Endsleigh Hotel to book a room for me for two nights, we had a self-service tea at the Strand Corner House. We had just left the building when Helen realized that she had left her gloves in the ladies' washroom. She dashed back for them and although it had been only a matter of minutes, they were gone.

Lyon's Corner Houses, where prices were reasonable and orchestras provided lovely background music, were very popular. In the self-service area, called the Salad Bowl, you could take as much as you liked and once, when I was there with John and David, they laughed at the amount I brought to the table.

As we had 'phoned several theatres from the Endsleigh without success, we took the tube to Golders Green to try the cinemas. Our seats were on the right of the train, with Helen was at the window and the narrow passage between me and the man on my left. He and I looked at each other, and, much to my amazement, there was instant recognition. He was a pleasant fellow called Bradshaw and I had last seen him in Yokohama where, working for Glen Line's Agent, Jardine, Matheson & Co. Ltd., he had come on board the *Glengarry*. I remembered that he had one of the new motor scooters which I first saw in Japan and also that he had said to me that he didn't think he was suited to the job. At any rate, he had only recently arrived home and was not returning to Japan. As he was in his twenties, I thought the middle-aged lady with him might be his mother, but he introduced her as his wife.

Having met with the same experience at the Golders Green cinemas as we had done with the central theatres, we travelled to Helen's lodgings at The Hall, 6A Primrose Hill Road, to allow her to change her clothes. And, after succeeding in getting into a news cinema, we had supper at the Strand Corner House before I saw her home and returned to the Endsleigh by taxi. It was 1am and, when I tipped the driver, his sarcastic remarks made it plain that it wasn't enough.

Sunday, 12 November, was Remembrance Sunday and, after breakfast, and yarning with some commercial travellers, I stood with them at the window watching a company of ATS marching to join the parade. The man next to me, however, was not impressed by the demeanour of the leading officer, who was striding out and swinging her arms high, as he commented, "I bet she's a right bitch."!
The Caledonian Christian Club was so close to the Endsleigh that I was able to spend some time with John before returning to the Hotel to meet Helen at 1pm. And, after lunch at the Hotel, we went down to the Victoria

Embankment and had a photographer take our picture beside Cleopatra's Needle, before boarding a train at Charing Cross Tube Station and heading for the ship.

With new floors being laid and almost every place locked up, the *Glengarry* was not looking her best. Even the wireless room was locked as the 2nd Sparks, whose name I can't recall, had left the key in his cabin and taken his cabin key ashore with him. As I had warned him not to do this, I was annoyed, but, as he was not sailing with me and the incident was over, I didn't make an issue of it. We had dinner on board, and, although it was about the poorest I had ever had, Helen tucked into a dish of mutton and said she enjoyed it. When Helen first saw the *Glengarry*, she jocularly remarked that it was "just a coble", but was impressed by her just the same and, when we saw the *Clytoneus* coming in as I was showing her round, we watched her manoeuvre towards her berth. It was nearly 6.30pm before we left the ship and, as the pass I had obtained for Helen expired at 5pm, the taxi I ordered to take us to Plaistow was unable to enter the dock and we had to walk to it at the gate. From Plaistow, we returned by tube to the City where we got 6/1d-seats (30p) in a cinema to see Bing Crosby in "Mr Music". Then, after supper in Lyon's in Piccadilly, I saw Helen home before returning to spend a second night at the Endsleigh.

Having risen and breakfasted early on Monday morning, it was only 8am when I called at the Club to tell John that I would meet him at Blackfriars Tube Station at 5pm. I then returned to spend the day on the *Glengarry* and also on the *Clytoneus* where I met I.T. Davies, the man I was to relieve. I travelled back to the City to meet John as arranged and after tea at the Strand Corner House, we spent the evening yarning at his club. He accompanied me to Kings Cross Tube Station where I caught a train for Plaistow and then a bus which took me along Connaught Road to the docks.

The Hall, in Primrose Hill, was a females only residence while the Caledonian Christian Club, in Endsleigh Gardens, was only for men. The Hall was nicer than the Club and more liberal in that it allowed men into the Common Room whereas ladies were not permitted to enter the Club. Once he had his bearings, John moved to digs in Hamlet Gardens, while Helen, who was happy at The Hall, remained there until she left London a year later. The Hall was full of young girls and Helen told me that when any of them asked what she should wear, the others would reply, "knickers and vest". And, on the first of the month, it was the superstitious rule that the first word uttered had to be "rabbits"!

On Tuesday morning, I received a message from Holts Dock Office telling me to 'phone Helen. When I did, she said she was going into Westminster Hospital in the afternoon to have a boil removed from under her arm and asked me to collect her at 4.30pm. On leaving the Hospital, we had tea at a Corner House and again visited a news cinema before I saw her home and returned to the ship.

John had got tickets from a lad at the Club for a dance organised by the students of Faraday House, the electrical engineering college. It was held at the Victoria Hall in Bloomsbury Square and, after collecting Helen at Primrose Hill and travelling by tube from Chalk Farm, we met up with John. The three of us were standing together when a girl approached us for a ladies' choice and, as fair-haired John was better looking than I was, I, and no doubt he, thought that she was coming for him. But, much to my surprise, she boosted my ego by choosing me!

The following day, Thursday, 16 November, 1950, I transferred my gear from the *Glengarry* to the *Clytoneus* (GMQG) and signed on the Articles.

29   COASTING THE CLYTONEUS

Bound for Antwerp, we sailed at 6.06am on Saturday, 18 November. 55-year-old Captain Peter Elder was Master and 34-year-old R.A. Hansell, who had been Mate of the *Atreus* with me in 1948, was Mate. Tall and pleasant 21-year-old Roy A. Simpson, the 2nd R/O, had also been on the *Atreus*, where, although only a supernumerary to Port Said, he had been very helpful. Mrs Elder, the Captain's wife, signed on as supernumerary.

The deck crowd were British while the engine room ratings and, with one exception, the stewards were Chinese. The exception was D.C. Dumbill who, although on the Articles as Assistant Steward, performed the duties of 2nd Steward to W. Cordrey, the Chief, as we had no 2nd Steward. Dumbill and I had been on the *Samnesse* together during her 11-month voyage in 1946/47 and I remembered him particularly for a betting incident in Durban and his speech to expats in Tanga.

I found our Surgeon, 24-year-old G. Smellie, a morose young man without conversation. This was his first trip to sea and, when I had occasion to visit him in his cabin on the crossing to Antwerp, he had his curtains drawn and was stretched out on his bunk.

We arrived off Flushing at 5pm on the same day we left London, but, due to the number of ships coming down the river from Antwerp, anchored in the Schelde for the night and it was 5pm on Sunday, 19 November before we docked.

I was ashore with Roy on both Sunday and Monday evenings. We didn't do anything more than walk about under the bright neon signs, but, in a dock-side tearoom, I met a young chap who had been at Wireless College in Dundee with me and who was on the North Atlantic run.

We left for Schiedam, near Rotterdam, at 2.42pm on Tuesday, 21 November, and, when we anchored in the vicinity of Ostend, it was blowing a gale and there was a distress on the air.

We arrived at 4.20am on Wednesday. The *Clytoneus* was to have her bottom scraped and, although I had been on ships in dry-dock before, this was my first experience of a floating one and I watched with interest as the water was pumped out of it to raise the ship out of the water. Being in dry-dock was always a nuisance as you had to go to a lavatory ashore.

I was ashore that morning to pay off an AB who was returning to his home in Colwyn Bay because his father had died. A taxi called for us at 8.30am and after we had collected the Agent at Meyer & Co.'s office in Rotterdam, the three of us walked to the Mercantile Marine Office, where the man signed off, before calling at Thomas Cook's and the British Consulate. Holts paid the AB's fare to Colwyn Bay plus 70 francs (10/- or 50p) expenses and I was most impressed by the service given by Cooks who told him where and when to change trains in Britain. The business was over by 10.15 and I bought a record of J'attendrai and three kilos of sugar before returning to the ship for lunch.

In the evening, Roy and I went to the Schiedam Mission as he wanted to buy some souvenirs there and the next morning I went into town on my own. A bottle of Advocaat, bought on a previous visit to the Netherlands, had been so enjoyed by my parents that I got them another one and also bought a doll on Roy's behalf.

I did not see Clare during our short visit, but 'phoned her from a dock office on Thursday afternoon. Because I was unfamiliar with the Dutch system, a man put the call through for me, but did not hand me the phone until he had ribbed Clare about me and had a good laugh. During our conversation, I asked Clare to recommend a record which would remind me of the Netherlands. She recommended 'Op de Woelige Baren' (On the Turbulent Waves/Sea) and I was able to get a recording of it, at G.P. van Daalen & Zoon's shop in Schiedam, sung by Eddy Christiani to the accompaniment of Frans Wouters and his Orchestra. The record became a favourite at home and, as the title contained the only words we memorized, we used to bawl them out when they appeared in the cheerful song.

In 1963, when she was engaged to be married, Clare moved to Spijkenisse where she had bought a house large enough to accommodate both her husband and herself and her aging parents. But, sadly, her fiancé, Nico, who had never complained of illness, died suddenly of a heart attack in September, 1964. After her 85-year-old father, already a widower, died, in 1973, she was left with only a cat for company. She invited me and my family to spend a holiday with her and, although we reciprocated, neither took up the offer. Early in 1994, when I didn't receive a calendar from her and my own was not acknowledged, I wrote asking if something were wrong. A reply came from a relative; Clare was now wandering in her mind and had been admitted to an old folk's home. I thought that this would be the last I would hear of her, but, in January, 2000, I received a communication informing me that Clare had died on 20 December, 1999 at the age of 83. And as the writer said, "The Lord has taken our dear niece, Klaasje Mol", it seems that her relatives are as religious as she was.

We sailed, for Hamburg, at 8.24pm on Thursday and, on arriving in the Elbe the following evening, anchored for the night as no ships were permitted to enter the port during darkness. We docked at 7.54am on Saturday, 25 November and, when mail arrived at noon, I received a letter from Helen and one from my father asking how my studying was getting on and if I might meet him again in London as he was going there the following week. I replied that my studying was at a standstill, that we were heading for Liverpool via Swansea, but if by any chance I ended up in London, he would have to make an appointment! I told Helen and my parents to address their next letters to the ship c/o T.H. Couch Ltd., 6/6a Wind Street, Swansea and sent my letters in Company's envelopes with the Blue Funnel logo on the back and under which I placed the ship's stamp –

CLYTONEUS
(Official No.) 182445
LIVERPOOL
4837 NET.

I didn't go ashore at all in Hamburg as, although we were alongside, it was a long journey by ferry down and across the river to Ste. Pauli and a further ten- minute tram ride to the centre. I explained this in my reply to my father and added "Apart from that, Hamburg, is a most uninspiring city in its present state and more so at this time of the year." It took years for the city to recover from the devastation caused by the RAF.

We sailed from Hamburg at 2pm on Thursday, 27 November and went out into the teeth of a gale which continued all the way to Swansea.

I had heard of Captain Elder from his nephew, Peter Bruce, who lived near me in Dundee and I also knew his sister-in-law. Although Captain Elder lived in Southport, he too came from Dundee and, when he came into my cabin one day, I almost mentioned that I knew Peter. I stopped myself, however, because he must have seen my birthplace and address on the Articles yet had made no reference to this.

Captain Elder subsequently became Holts Nautical Adviser and his elder son, also Peter, who joined the Company in 1953, became a Master, Assistant Marine Superintendent at Gladstone Dock and finally Operations Manager. His other son, Graham, also served with Holts and became manager of McGregor Cory in Cricklewood.

Peter Bruce and I had travelled to Canada together on the *Queen Elizabeth* in July, 1943 when he was going to train with the RAF and I was to join *Liberty Ship 'D'* which turned out to be the *Samite*. The last time I saw Peter was when, as at student at Edinburgh University in the late 1950s, I alighted from the train one summer's evening at Aberdour in Fife. He spotted me on the platform and, leaning out of the door before the train continued its journey to Dundee, said that he worked for DC Thomson, but was now emigrating to Canada, the country he had already visited under very different circumstances.

Mrs Elder was a bad sailor and didn't appear for meals all the way from Hamburg to Swansea. She stood beside me at the rail, however, as we were passing the Longships Light House, off Landsend, on the evening of Wednesday, 29 November and said that, although she had not been seasick, she knew that she would have been if she had not lain on her bunk taking Kwells. She also commented that her husband had said that she would have bedsores if she remained in bed any longer!

Due to the weather, the speed of the 16-knot 'A' Class *Clytoneus* was reduced, at times, to 10 knots so that it was 9.21am on Thursday, the 30th, before we docked in Swansea. Mail awaited our arrival and I didn't go ashore that day, but spent the evening writing a long overdue letter to the ROU regarding my subscriptions.

As Captain and Mrs Elder, all the Mates, the Surgeon and the Bosun were paying off, I was kept busy on Friday morning; flying round in a taxi to the Agents and the Mercantile Marine Office. The Mates, who left to go home on leave, were Hansell, A. MacKenzie, 2nd Mate, then 29 and who retired as Master in 1980, C. Woolley, 3rd Mate, and C.L. Pielow, 4th Mate.

Dr Smellie was accompanying the Bosun, 44-year-old H. Hand, to Liverpool where he was to enter the hospital for rare tropical diseases. Mr Hand had been ill since Rotterdam where his joints had begun to swell before large red spots appeared on his legs. The disease, apparently very rare, was not infectious.

The replacements signed on were G.F. Bonham, Master, R.B. Tiplady, 1st Mate, T.W. Willows, 2nd Mate, P.A. Leighton, 3rd Mate, W.E. Ligertwood, 4th Mate, J.Sanders, Bosun and Mrs M.L. McIntyre,

Supernumerary and wife of W. McIntyre, the 29-year-old 2nd Engineer. Ship's business took me to the Mercantile Marine Office and to the office of T.H. Couch Ltd, our Agent, a number of times. Everyone was friendly and obliging but, with its high stools and antiquated furniture, the latter's office was so out of date that it was like entering a world which had existed fifty years earlier.

Captain Bonham was a small slim man in his fifties and, although he was considered a martinet and what I had heard of him was not favourable, I got on fine with him. Tiplady, whom I had already met on the *Eurybates*, was kind enough to say to me that some of the newer pursers were not so efficient!

Swansea was still badly scarred by the bombing it had received during the war, but I liked the city and was impressed by the covered market where all sorts of produce was sold. On Saturday evening, I went with Roy, Peter Leighton, and Bill Ligertwood, to a dance in Oystermouth and on Sunday afternoon Roy and I went to the Mumbles. Double-decker trains, which looked more like trams, ran round the bay from Swansea to the Mumbles and, after spending some time there, we walked back into Oystermouth by the hill road to board a return train. The train service round that lovely bay has long been discontinued, but I still have a South Wales Transport Co., Ltd. ticket as a souvenir and have met a lady who claims to have the last ticket sold.

For me, that visit to the Mumbles was a mark of respect for all those who died on that wild night in April, 1947 when the *Samtampa* broke up on rocks off Sker Point. All hands were lost; together with the entire crew of Mumbles Lifeboat which went to their assistance.

I had not before, when coasting, been required to make up the wage accounts of the British crew at the end of a voyage, but spent all day Wednesday doing this and worked till midnight in order to post them off to Liverpool next day. Daily and not monthly rates were applied to coastal voyages and cash drawn at ports and Steward's Accounts had to be deducted. As the Chinese were on separate Foreign Articles, no accounts had to be made out for them.

Roy and I went to a dance at the Mission (Missions to Seamen) on Thursday evening. A service was held during the interval and, when a group of Lascar (Indian) seamen asked me if they could go as they were Roman Catholics, I said it would be OK. Everyone, except me and a

Norwegian seaman, attended the service and when he was asked why he didn't go, he said "Me like dance."!

On returning from the dance I wrote in answer to a letter received that day from my mother. I wanted to see Australia before I gave up the sea, but, knowing that I wanted a job at home, she had enclosed an advert in the Dundee Courier for a clerical position at Kings Cross Hospital. I had replied immediately to the advert and received a reply from the doctor in charge asking me to come for interview. But, as he disclosed the wage and it was too low, I wrote and told him so. I then got a nice reply saying that he quite understood, but that it was not in his power to increase it.

It was again blowing hard when we sailed at 1am on Friday, 8 December and, although the Lynas pilot boat was on station, off Anglesey, and the pilot boarded at 5pm, the boat had been damaged in the gale. We docked in Vittoria Dock, Birkenhead at 12.30pm on Saturday and I spent the evening at a dance in St Stephen's Church Hall.

I crossed by ferry to Liverpool on Sunday. A performance of Handel's 'Messiah' was being given at the Philharmonic Hall and, as it was getting near Christmas, I wondered if I'd have the luck to spend it at home. But, when I 'phoned Calverley on Monday morning, he said that I would probably be joining the *Calchas* (GMSS) in London for another voyage to the Far East!

Customs had boarded on our arrival and goods on which duty was paid were put into bond until the day we wished to take them out of the docks. In my case this was nylon stockings and, after we signed off on Monday afternoon, I collected them before making, with my suitcase and grip, for India Buildings for instructions from Calverley. And thankfully, as I had no wish to return to the Far East, I learned that I was being spared the *Calchas* and was to join the *Glenroy* (GPPN) in London to coast her to Middlesbrough.

When I went to book in at Atlantic House, there was a crowd at the desk and it was obvious that all the rooms were taken. A girl was on the 'phone and, when she turned to the man in front of me and asked, "For one?", I deduced she was booking a room elsewhere for him, held up two fingers and she said "Two"! I had no idea where I was going, but it turned out to be Plimsoll House. My new acquaintance, a young engineer, and I walked there together and shared a room for the night.

On my return to India Buildings in the morning, I found that Calverley had changed his mind. I was to take the *Glenaffaric* (GDPS) round to London and then on to Hamburg to be sold. One minute I was envisaging another Christmas in the East and the next, in Middlesbrough or Hamburg! But, when I went once more to India Buildings on Wednesday morning, expecting to be told to join the *Glenaffaric*, Calverley had again changed his mind and said, "How would you like the *Deucalion*? She's going to Australia." I hastily accepted, but he went on to say that the *Ixion* (MLLB), fitting out in Belfast, would be ready next month and that Reg Peaston, who was to sail as her 1st RO/Purser, was ill and that, if he hadn't recovered, I could have her. It was all too good to be true and, as the *Ixion* was, similar to the *Helenus*, one of the large 'H' Class which did 18 knots and carried twenty-nine first-class passengers, I hoped that Mr Peaston's illness would linger awhile! It would be great to be on the *Ixion* for her maiden voyage. But, in any case, I was to join the *Deucalion* (GDQW) in Glasgow and coast her to Liverpool.

Postscript: The *Clytoneus*, a Mark 2 'A' Class ship built at the Caledon Yard in Dundee in 1948, went to breakers in Kaohsiung, Taiwan in 1973. Like so many others similarly disposed of, she was good for years of further service, but containerisation, and the convenience of air travel, had made their design obsolete.

Other seafaring books by Ian M. Malcolm

LIFE ON BOARD A WARTIME LIBERTY SHIP (print and ebook formats, published by Amberley)

Describes the author's wartime experiences as the 3rd Radio Officer of the Liberty Ships *Samite* and *Samforth*.

OUTWARD BOUND (print and ebook formats, published by Moira Brown)

The author's first post-war voyage; on the Liberty Ship *Samnesse*, managed by Blue Funnel for the Ministry of Transport. The voyage begins with calls at Piraeus and Genoa, after which months are spent tramping to various ports in East Africa and the Red Sea. A very happy ship with a predominantly young crew basking in the post-war euphoria.

BACK TO SEA (print and ebook formats, published by Moira Brown)

A voyage to the Far East on the 1911-built *Atreus*, which carries pilgrims to Jeddah on her homeward passage. The author then attends the Lifeboat School in Liverpool and stands by the 1928-built *Eurybates* in Belfast before making his first two voyages on Glen Line's *Glengarry*.

LAST VOYAGE AND BEYOND (print and ebook formats, published by Moira Brown)

The Australian part of the voyage, on *Deucalion* (built in 1920 as the *Glenogle*) proves enjoyable, but is followed by a trip round Indonesian islands, loading copra, which, although a most interesting experience, is not. On returning home, the author spends two unhappy years in a Dundee office after which he works at GPO Coast Stations for three years, before resigning to train as a teacher in Edinburgh.

SHIPPING COMPANY LOSSES OF THE SECOND WORLD WAR (print and ebook formats, published by the History Press)

Describes the losses suffered by 53 companies in detail; giving masters' names, where bound, convoy numbers, positions when sunk, casualties and enemy involved.

LETTERS FROM A RADIO OFFICER (print and ebook formats, published by Moira Brown)

Letters sent to the author from a former shipmate who, from 1951 till 1963, served with Brocklebank, Marconi, Redifon (ashore and afloat), the Crown Agents, Clan Line, the Royal Fleet Auxiliary (RFA), Ferranti (in Edinburgh), and Marconi again before settling for a shore job in London.

DANGEROUS SEAS (print and ebook formats, published by Moira Brown)

Four book collection – *Dangerous Voyaging, Dangerous Voyaging 2, Fortunes of War* and *Mined Coasts*.

The reader will be left in no doubt of the sacrifices made by the men, and also a few women, of the wartime Merchant Navy.

Printed in Great Britain
by Amazon